Golfing with
the Master

Phil Callaway

HARVEST HOUSE PUBLISHERS

EUGENE, OREGON

Cover by Left Coast Design, Portland, Oregon

Cover photo © Murray & Associates, Inc. / Picturesque, Inc. / Workbook.com

GOLFING WITH THE MASTER
Copyright © 2006 by Phil Callaway
Published by Harvest House Publishers
Eugene, Oregon 97402
www.harvesthousepublishers.com

Library of Congress Cataloging-in-Publication Data
Callaway, Phil, 1961-
    Golfing with the Master / Phil Callaway.
    p. cm.
    ISBN 978-0-7369-1720-9 (pbk.)
    1. Golfers—Religious life. 2. Golf—Religious life—Christianity. I. Title.
    BV4596. G64C34 2006
    242'.68—dc22   2005031528

Printed in the United States of America

09 10 11 12 13 14 15 16 / BP-MS / 12 11 10 9 8 7 6 5 4

Advance Applause for
Golfing with the Master...

"*Golfing with the Master* will enrich not only your outlook on golf but also your outlook on life. It's filled with great, homespun golf humor and enough personal experiences to keep you smiling for a week. Most importantly, it will help all golfers develop a stronger personal relationship with Jesus on and off the course."

Wally Armstrong
PGA tour player, teacher, and author of *The Heart of a Golfer*

"This book is a kick in the pants! Phil Callaway transitions seamlessly from the golf course to everyday life. One minute, he gets me carefully considering my faith, and the next minute he's got me laughing out loud! I highly recommend this book."

Casey Martin
PGA tour player

"Playing golf with Phil Callaway is almost as much fun as reading this book. I laughed. I almost cried. I even forgot about my score. And when I least expected it, I learned something. If you're anything like me, you'll want to keep several copies of this book in your golf bag for inspiration. Or to give out to people when you forget to yell 'Fore!'"

Ken Davis
bestselling author and speaker

"I've golfed with Phil, and he needs money for lessons. So buy armloads of this book. Give them out to friends and complete strangers. Amid the laughter they'll discover timeless principles that will change their game and their lives."

Mike Yorkey
coauthor of the Every Man's Battle series

"Making sense of my golf game is like trying to understand the purpose of pain. Golf can be enraging, humiliating, and exhilarating all at once. I make just enough good shots to keep me coming back for more. I hoped this book would help me make sense of my golf game, but it healed something far deeper. Plain and simple—'Philosopher Phil' provides helpful insights on the emotional and spiritual sides of life. This is a must-read for anyone trying to grasp the meaning of life as seen through the game of golf."

Joel Freeman
motivational speaker, author, and former chaplain of the Washington Bullets

"The majority of my life I've been a competitive person learning life lessons from the game of hockey. Phil Callaway has shown me how the game of golf (another favorite of mine) demonstrates patience, perseverance, and integrity—all characteristics God desires in our life. This book is an entertaining read that will have you laughing out loud (except for his comments on hockey in chapter 2!) while challenging you with the things that matter most."

Shane Doan
captain of NHL's Phoenix Coyotes

"Even if you think playing golf is a bit less fun than mall-walking, you're about to gain a new appreciation of the sport. Funny things happen to Phil when he plays golf, and he has a great time telling of his adventures and misadventures—whether playing on a homemade course or an actual course with flagsticks and everything. But beyond the humor and the tongue-in-cheek insistence that golf is the greatest sport on earth (has Phil never played basketball?), Callaway intersperses his lightheartedness with a healthy helping of biblical truth and godly wisdom. Each story points the reader toward a life of Christlikeness and faith—something every duffer who ever drowned a golf ball can pursue."

Dave Branon
writer for SportsSpectrum.com and *Our Daily Bread*

"Phil's golf stories will touch the heart of every golfer, but his spiritual message is the best of all."

Bearcat Murray
member of NHL's Calgary Flames

"Phil Callaway finds ways to push life lessons through a tunnel of laughter. My funny bone gets tickled even while I'm focused on the game Mark Twain suggested was little more than 'a good walk ruined.'"

Ryan Walter
sports broadcaster, Stanley Cup champion

This book is dedicated to the Circle of Six.
Better golfers you will find.
But better friends? It is doubtful.
Thanks for checking my scorecard,
for enduring my pranks,
and for sharpening my irons.

Contents

The Invitation

Let's pretend that one day along about the middle of July, your spouse (if you have one) hands you the cordless and says, "It's Tiger—Tiger Woods." You are sipping lemonade at the time and lounging in a hammock you purchased on sale at Wal-Mart when it dropped below 20 bucks. Taking the phone, you jam it to your ear and say, "Yeah right, who is this, and what do you want?"

Silence. Then you hear a laugh you've heard on TV. You picture a grin you've seen while he hoists major trophies above his head.

"Will you golf with me?" asks Tiger. "We tee off at one PM."

"Um…uh…" you stammer. "Well, ahem—"

"It's just me and a few friends."

"F-f-friends?" Your tongue will not cooperate.

Amid the shock, you hear him mention a few of his buddies. Some guys named Arnold and Jack. He says the three of them just want to hang out a bit. Get to know you.

"Where do we land the helicopter?" he asks.

You are having trouble responding for two reasons: There is lemonade up your nose. And you have fallen out of the blasted hammock.

"Uh, you can land it at the hospital," you manage. "I'll meet you there. I think I'm having a heart attack."

Ridiculous, you say. That could never happen. And you're probably right. The odds of Tiger calling your house today are the same as the odds of being hit by a falling coconut in Nome, Alaska. After all, a master of the game of golf wouldn't stoop to play with the likes of us, would he?

Well, I have bad news and I have good news. The bad news is that you might be right about Tiger. But the good news is that the Master of all creation has extended you an invitation to walk with Him. He has your picture in His wallet; He has a tee time booked with you. The Bible says, "Long before he laid down earth's foundations, he had us in mind, had settled on us as the focus of his love" (Ephesians 1:4 MSG).

This past winter, thanks to our Uncle Air Miles, our family enjoyed the sand and surf of Maui (if you're reading this in Moose Lake, Yukon, I apologize) and a brief visit to the Mercedes Open. The world's best had assembled there to shoot it out for the coveted trophy. Or maybe it was the million dollars.

Few times in my life have I enjoyed myself more. But while

I've been privileged to stand on some of the world's most magnificent golf courses, I cannot do so without a tugging in my soul. That tugging prompted me to spend 90 mornings this summer immersing myself in the Gospel accounts. Underlining. Meditating on the words of Jesus. After the immersing, I would call my sons or some friends, and we would head out to the course, where we would golf and tell stories. It wasn't easy, all this research. But three things happened:

First, I got golfer's tan. I sit in the swimming pool now, and teenagers wrinkle their pierced eyebrows at my leathery neck, my tanned legs, and what appear to be little white socks.

Second, I shaved four strokes from my handicap with a few simple tips I'll be happy to show you.

And best of all, I came to understand 36 life principles this glorious game can teach us. Principles that are essential to getting our lives back on course.

I'd love to offer you a cordless phone with a direct link to Tiger. But I have something far better to share with you today. The Master wants to walk with you. He wants to be your teacher and your coach. He wants to lead you beside still waters, all the way Home.

So thanks for joining me. Grab your clubs. Looks like we're up.

1

The Call of the Mild

Golf, like the measles, should be caught young, for, if postponed to riper years, the results may be serious.
P.G. WODEHOUSE

Golf is so popular simply because it is the best game in the world at which to be bad.
A.A. MILNE

I've about had it with winter. It's the middle of April, and dirty brown snowdrifts are still smothering the garden and choking the life out of the tulips. The thermometer claims it's 36 degrees. That's being generous. Winter keeps coming back like my childhood dentist when he poked his head into the waiting room, looking for victims.

I've done all I can to ease the pain. I putt in the living room; I chip onto the sofa. I've even bought a coffee table book: *100 Courses You Can Play*—knowing I can't play a one of them.

On the windward side of the Hawaiian Island of Oahu is the Koolau golf course. It mocks me from the colorful pages of the book. Considered by many to be the toughest course on earth, Koolau is set within an ancient volcano. Locals have dubbed it King Kong in a grass skirt. Monster Mash. Beauty and the Beast. Bring twice as many balls as you have strokes in your handicap, they advise. The course record is 69. Lost balls, that is.

I don't care. I'd golf the Sahara right now. Sand traps aren't that bad. Bring it on. Christopher Columbus went around the world in 1492. That's not a bad score when you think about it.

I phone my friends Vance and Ron. "I can't take it any more," I whine. "I'm pulling my clubs out of cold storage. Let's go."

The clubhouse is dark and vacant when we arrive. Jim, the course manager, is busily repairing the bridge that crosses the creek to the first tee. I chat with him about the level of the creek, about his family, about Christmas. But he knows why I'm here. I'm like a bird dog pointing at the first tee. Surely lifers like myself can get on a wee bit early, I plead. He laughs and points at the fairway on two. There's a lake on it large enough to attract a floatplane, he says. You go out there and we'll have to form a search party.

I glance over at Vance and Ron, who are waiting patiently

in the van, their noses pressed against the frosty glass. I can't quite tell, but I think they're drooling.

"How about a bucket of range balls?" I beg, hoping Jim will throw me some scraps.

"Sure," he smirks. "Just don't slip on the skating rink there on the left."

We cross the bridge expectantly, each of us lugging a well-rounded bucket. Long months of winter fade into memory as we trudge through the muck, laughing like little children on Christmas morning. Tired golf jokes are funny once more. The clouds overhead scatter, allowing the sun to poke through. Silver linings are everywhere.

"See that sand trap by the 150-yard marker?" I point.

"That's no sand trap, that's a snowdrift."

"Come on. Use your imaginations. Let's try to hit it," says Vance.

"Okay, you shoot a ball, then it's my turn," says Ron.

"We'll shoot until someone lands in the trap. Loser hits the rest of his bucket with his shirt off."

I'm not worried. I can beat these guys with my eyes closed. The first day of the year my golf game is together. My swing hasn't had time to know any better. There's a little rust on it, a little frost, but since I have no expectations of doing well, I am usually tremendous. I tee one up and chip it toward the snow trap, tingling with anticipation at the long summer stretching before me.

Watching the ball take flight, I remember why I love this game.

There's the wonder of majestic scenery, of course. But it goes far deeper.

I love the stillness out here and the talks with my sons as we look for my ball.

I love the smell of fresh mown grass and the reminder that life is a walk, not a sprint.

I love the way golf brings my sins bubbling to the surface like no other sport, reminding me of bad habits I need to work on.

I love the amusing grace of a mulligan.

I love the way this game has begun to teach me humility.

I love the camaraderie of a Texas Scramble, of best ball. Perhaps it's the closest some of us get to a church. We care about the other guy's swing; we cheer each other on.

I love the discipline of working at something I know I can improve upon.

I love the hope I feel before each swing.

I even love the embarrassment of forgetting I have golf shoes on and standing at the checkout line in our small town's one and only grocery store with little kids pointing at the "funny old man" who writes those books.

And now that I think about it, I don't even mind winter so much. Maybe next year I'll make a concerted effort to complain less. To change my attitude. It's one of the best clubs you can have in your bag, I'm told.

They say God's faithfulness is like the seasons. That "as long as the earth remains, there will be springtime and harvest, cold and heat, winter and summer, day and night" (Genesis 8:22). It's the hope every April golfer clings to where I come from. Springtime is a reminder that God's mercies are new every morning, that His faithfulness is unending, that He hasn't failed us yet.

These thoughts have me smiling right now. I don't even mind losing to these guys. I'll finish this bucket and then put on my shirt.

—⚏—

For the LORD is good. His unfailing love continues forever, and his faithfulness continues to each generation.

PSALM 100:5

Question of the Day: How have I seen God's faithfulness in the past year?

Tip of the Day: Always warm up. If time is short, forget the range. Instead, chip and putt. Swing two clubs together 20 times. Starting two feet from the cup, drop four balls a foot apart. Move out a foot only when you sink one. This way you can save three dollars a day on driving range balls. In the average lifetime that's more than $87,000 (if you golf every day from the day you were born).

2

A Christian Game

Drugs are very much a part of professional
sports today, but when you think about it,
golf is the only sport where the players aren't
penalized for being on grass.
BOB HOPE

I wish I was better at golf.
BOXER ARTURO GATTI TO HIS WIFE AS HE WAITED
FOR MEDICAL TREATMENT FOLLOWING A BLOODY
TEN-ROUND BATTLE

Golf is, quite simply, the greatest game on earth. This is not
up for debate. But just in case there are two or three doubters,
allow me to submit the following irrefutable truths.

Golf is a Christian game, requiring of its players honesty,
self-control, meekness, faith, hope, perseverance, and long-
suffering. The rules of golf reprimand ill behavior, including

swearing, cheating, chewing tobacco, coveting your friend's clubs, throwing your clubs, or throwing your friend's clubs. As if this weren't proof enough, golf is played in a garden, where God intended men and women to be from the beginning.

Here are six examples of pastimes that some people believe to be in the same league as golf. As you will see, these people are dead wrong.

1. Boxing

Technically, anything that cannot be played with your close friends does not qualify as an actual sport. Does the world heavyweight champion really enjoy beating up on a buddy? Except for a few noteworthy exceptions, I don't think so. Unlike golf, you cannot discuss important issues while you are boxing, nor can you pick up your teeth while wearing a boxing glove.

2. Hockey

Though I have played ice hockey since the age of three, hockey is too rough to qualify as an actual sport. You will find it in the dictionary under *war*. Hockey has no winners—only survivors. I have broken several bones playing this game, including my nose and jaw, and have been knocked unconscious and still suffer memory loss. I also suffer memory loss. When a defense-man misses a check, the goalie can cover for him. Not in golf. When a player goes offside, he does not stop the play and tell others what

Now you know... The first time Western Open tournament director Peter deYoung played golf with Michael Jordan, the basketball superstar stroked a 20-foot putt that lipped the cup but stayed out. DeYoung picked up the ball and flipped it back to him. Jordan tossed the ball at the cup from 20 feet away. "Not only did it go in," deYoung recalls, "it stayed in."

he has done. There are scores of other reasons hockey is not a sport, but my head hurts when I try to remember them.

3. Soccer

I am sorry, soccer fanatics, but this pastime is not technically a sport. It is a religion. My friend James grew up in Germany, where people bow down at soccer shrines daily. Soccer fans are more violent than the players. The net is huge and the field is too large. There are guys with poor eyesight on soccer fields around the world, running in circles for hours after the game, faithfully playing their positions and yelling for the ball, unaware that the fans have gone home. You cannot do this in golf. Golfers must have good eyesight because the ball is so small. If you run around after dark on the golf course, you will fall into the creek.

4. Football

How can football qualify as a sport when the ball won't even roll straight? When you have to confer with others before each play? When you wait for the referees to tell you when the TV advertisements are over? Although I appreciate the fact that the players huddle for prayer before each play, this is not a Christian game. There are less than four minutes of action in a three-hour game. Which makes me think of another "sport."

5. Baseball

Nothing happens in baseball. Center fielders have fallen asleep during games, and the sad thing is, no one noticed. The umpires do not carry watches; they carry calendars. Players who nap in the dugout self-administer smelling salts before a trip to the on-deck circle. Every pitcher is a "scratch" pitcher. In baseball you can take a player out if he's having a bad game.

Not in golf. In baseball you get unlimited foul balls. Even I would be a professional if allowed to do this in golf. In baseball you can hit a home run over right, left, or center field. In golf every shot must be straight over second base.

6. Tennis

I enjoy the exercise tennis provides, but it is not a sport. The rules of tennis are annoyingly uncomplicated. Tennis players are not devoted enough to play the game on hot summer afternoons or in rainstorms. Grunting while hitting the ball is simply not acceptable in golf.

My son read my list above and grinned. He said, "Dad, golf is far more boring to watch than baseball." I told him I would pray for him. Apparently he agreed with the poor soul who said, "If you want to take long walks, take long walks. If you want to hit things with sticks, hit things with sticks. But there's no excuse for combining the two and putting the results on TV. Golf is not so much a sport as an insult to lawns."

So I reminded my son of a few more reasons golf is the greatest game on earth. With these, I rest my case:

- PGA events don't feature loud music between shots.
- My son plays golf with people four times his age.
- Most golfers do not need a referee.
- Tickets to see Tiger are $30. Tickets for hockey are $200. More for football.
- Tiger signs balls he almost kills people with. Hockey players don't sign pucks that go into the crowd.
- You can bring a picnic basket to a PGA event. Try this at a football game.

- Having generated a billion dollars since 1938, the PGA is the only professional sports organization designed to donate its net proceeds from tournaments to local charities. I like that.

- You can play golf with your grandchildren. And beat them. I like that too.

- In golf, every shot is a new beginning.

- I have played many sports poorly. None is as satisfying to fail at as golf.

- When all else fails, golf has the mulligan.

I submit to you, my friend, that golf is a Christian game.

—∾—

Teach me your way, O Lord; lead me in a straight path.

PSALM 27:11 NIV

Question of the Day: In what way does golf remind me of my spiritual journey?

Tip of the Day: Work out whenever possible. Depending on your age this may mean juggling barbells or squeezing the remote. But be active. One great exercise for golfers is simple sit-ups. They strengthen your lower back, something every golfer needs. Younger guys can do sit-ups while juggling barbells.

3

What Drives You?

I'm a golfaholic, no question about that.
Counseling wouldn't help me. They'd have
to put me in prison, and then I'd talk the
warden into building a hole or two and
teach him how to play.
LEE TREVINO

Some of us worship in churches,
some in synagogues, some on golf courses.
ADLAI STEVENSON

One of the dangers of writing a book about a recreational game like golf is that people begin accusing you of doing nothing else with your time. They think you get up each morning, shed your Tiger Woods pajamas, adjust your golf ball tie, cruise to work in a car with the bumper sticker "I'd rather be driving a golf ball," and then tape a note to your office door that says, "Gone fishing for golf balls."

"Years ago," they mumble to each other, "when tribes thumped the ground with clubs, yelled loudly, and cursed, it was called witchcraft. Today, we call it golf."

Perhaps they have a point. For some people, golf has become an obsession. They'd play Mount Everest if someone put a flagstick on it. I even heard about a guy whose wife can't stand it when he tees off before eight in the morning. He uses a lob wedge from the living room carpet and last time hit a lamp.

After writing *With God on the Golf Course*, I received some marvelous mail from golf nuts. But I also found that some people out there—good, law-abiding citizens—view golfers with all the warmth they normally reserve for tax auditors (except that they believe tax auditors are useful people).

Here's one of those letters:

> I've been married to a golf nutsoid for 21 years and I've about had enough. He plays golf five times a week and when he comes home he watches it. Then he reads about it. We're having dinner with friends and it always comes up. In the past, my son kept me company when his dad was playing golf, but now he goes with him. Last week my husband showed up with a gift for me. I was so excited until I opened it. I can't believe they make a What Would Tiger Do? bracelet. I think they call it golf because all the other four-letter words were taken. When I die, you can bury me on the golf course. It's the only way my husband will visit. What should I do? Don't you dare tell me to start playing golf!

I think she signed it Frosted in Florida.

If you are Frosted's husband, I'm glad you're reading this book. Here's how to tell if you have a problem. You know you're a golfaholic when...

- You are playing golf and it is raining.
- You are unable to count past five.
- You are playing golf and it is snowing.
- Lightning only encourages you.
- You are playing golf and it is Christmas morning.
- Or your twenty-fifth anniversary.
- You live to shoot your age.
- You live to shoot your weight.

I hate to be the one to break it to you, but there is more to life than golf. I am not saying this because I lost a match this morning and I'm a little ornery (though both may be the case). Believe me, few people on earth enjoy the game of golf more than I do. I love to watch a 30-foot putt break sharply to the left, spin around the cup, and drop (I have seen this happen on television). But if golf is the high point of your life, you are stockpiling regrets. If golf garners your highest allegiance, you will come up empty.

When the wise men brought their gifts to Jesus in Matthew chapter two, they "fell down before him and worshiped him." Only one is worthy of our worship. He is the King of kings and the Lord of lords.

> **Now you know...** After Bruce Lietzke's children were born, he admitted that golf wasn't even in his top five priorities. He spent his summers coaching his three children's baseball teams and still managed to win 13 tournaments from 1970 through 1995.

So I have two recommendations. The first is this: Break your clubs. Okay, I'm kidding. But you may want to give your clubs a break. This will allow you time to think about my second suggestion: Get a grip.

By his own admission, Greg Norman self-destructed on the final few holes of the 1996 Masters. Yet he held it in perspective. "I screwed up," he said. "It's all on me. I know that. But losing this Masters is not the end of the world. I let this one get away, but I still have a pretty good life. I'll wake up tomorrow still breathing, I hope. All these hiccups I have, they must be for a reason. All this is just a test. I just don't know what the test is yet."

I spent some time recently with Rick Warren, author of *The Purpose-Driven Life*, a book that has sold a couple of copies here and there. Rick believes we are all driven by something. Some of us are driven by the need to drive golf balls. Others by the desire to win or the fear of losing. Still others are driven by the quest for stuff, the need for approval, or by resentment, anger, and guilt.

But when we discover a deeper purpose, real life begins. Nothing can compare with the joy of fulfilling the purpose for which we were created. Nothing can compensate for not discovering it.

When our children were small, the president of a large company called, offering me a job at triple the salary we now earn in an area of the country where I could golf all year round.

God had never spoken this clearly to me before.

I held the phone close to my ear and said rapidly, "Let me pray about it there I prayed about it." I'm not dumb. I checked it out. But I soon discovered the job would require more of my time than I was willing to give. It would mean turning my back on family and pursuing fame. Saying no was a turning point in my life. From that day forward I've tried to pursue my purpose in life:

- Walk close to Jesus every day.
- Build a strong marriage.
- Love my kids.
- Perform meaningful work.
- Make others homesick for heaven.

Knowing my purpose has given life meaning and substance. It has simplified things. I no longer make decisions based on guilt or outside pressure. I ask, "Will this help me fulfill God's purpose for my life?" Knowing my purpose has focused and motivated me. I am not here for long (just ask my hair), so what I do today matters.

Have you noticed that sports have slogans now? The National Hockey League ad goes like this: "Hockey that matters." The NBA has one: "I love this game." Major League Baseball came along and took it one step further: "I live for this." Now, I love baseball (despite what I told you in chapter two), but if I live for it, I have short-circuited my God-given wiring. I was made for more than this.

Buried deep in my shed is a small box of trophies. An MVP hockey trophy, several small golf awards, some tennis medals, and baseball stuff.

A few are broken.

All will one day rust.

Isn't it a little odd that we expend so much of our energy on the brief blip of the temporary while forgetting the eternal?

One day soon I will stand before God, and He will tally up my scorecard. The Bible says, "Remember, each of us will stand personally before the judgment seat of God…Yes, each of us will have to give a personal account to God" (Romans 14:10, 12). I will not be asked to divulge my handicap or display those rusting trophies. Instead I will hear one vital question: "What did you do with My grace?"

Until then the game of golf will be an opportunity, not an obsession. An opportunity to exercise and rest and build relationships. An opportunity to share my faith.

Now I'd better go repair that lamp.

—〰—

He died for everyone so that those who receive his new life will no longer live to please themselves. Instead, they will live to please Christ.

2 CORINTHIANS 5:15

Question of the Day: What is my definition of success?

Tip of the Day: Learn to avoid the ground when teeing off. Jack Nicklaus once said, "Through years of experience I have found that air offers less resistance than dirt." If trying to claim the Largest Divot prize in a tournament, the recommended club is a 6-iron.

4

Get Back

*Duffers who consistently shank
their balls are urged to buy and study
Shanks—No Thanks by R.K. Hoffman,
or in extreme cases, M.S. Howard's
excellent Tennis for Beginners.*
HENRY BEARD

*I want the same discipline in my
faith that I have in my golf game.*
SCOTT SIMPSON

A guy I know watches the Golf Channel religiously, pursuing the perfect club, stalking the latest innovation that will somehow offer him hope for his hook—something he prefers to call a draw. He called me once in the dead of winter, ecstatic about something he found on eBay. A revolutionary iron or a new set of power grips—I can't remember.

After the snow melted, we enjoyed a round together, and

he proudly showed me two recent purchases: a fairway 7-wood and a belly putter. The clubs had given him confidence that he would break 100 this year, he said. But as the round progressed, it became clear that the only way this guy would break 100 was to quit after 11 holes. The clubs had failed him. His game was in the tank.

When he lined up for each shot, he looked as if he were getting ready to parachute behind enemy lines. His hook was so bad that he faced the sixth fairway when shooting at the eighth. Attempting to remedy the problem, he employed stances he has seen on television: the open stance, the closed stance, and a new one—the bowlegged stance. He looked like a caveman killing his dinner.

Now you must understand that one of Callaway's First Rules of Golf (after "Never comment on other people's outfits") is "Never offer advice unless you're asked," so I bit my tongue each time he took a swing. Finally, with a few frustrating shots to go, he sought my opinion. I reminded him that I'm no expert and then simply said, "I think you shouldn't use your putter off the tee. Try a 3-wood." He didn't think this was funny. I said, "I think you need to return to basics."

Now you know… From 1979 to 1988, Seve Ballesteros won three British Opens, two Masters, and six European money titles. But in an effort to regain his youthful vigor, he unwisely consulted with scores of highly paid swing doctors. The muddled advice left him with such a wild swing that in the 1995 Ryder Cup, his teammates could barely watch when he stepped up to swat his tee shots.

When he asked what I meant, I reminded him of Vince Lombardi, the legendary Green Bay Packers coach. When the Packers lost a game due to mistakes, Lombardi would hold a football high above his head at the next practice. "Gentlemen," he would say, "this is a football."

"Practice the fundamentals," I told him. "Stick to basics. Don't torture your mind with a thousand thoughts. Spend time checking your grip, your aim, and your alignment. The hottest driver on the market or the next generation golf ball won't help you a hill of beans if you don't work on the basics."

"Okay," he said, and commenced to smack another one into the creek.

Contrast this guy's golf with two college students who invited me to teach them this glorious and frustrating game.

I still don't know why they asked me. Apparently they'd heard I could play golf reasonably well, and I wasn't about to inform them otherwise. But on the way to the course I began to question my wisdom. I began to feel unequipped for the task—like I was bringing a cap gun to a shootout at the OK Corral. After all, the game of golf is a complex one. You can do a hundred and twelve things right and then lift your head, and—*splat!*—you're in the creek. Where shall I start with these two?

You already know the answer. Go back to basics.

One of the beginners had all the right gear. A gorgeous set of clubs. Golf shoes. Sunglasses. A black Nike glove. The only equipment the other student had was borrowed from me.

We headed to the driving range with three buckets of balls.

John Halliwell, a golf-teaching friend of mine, has two rules about teaching golf. (1) You can't pay me. (2) Don't complain when you get your money's worth.

Employing both rules from the start, I acquainted them with the proper stance and grip. But they weren't interested. They wanted to hit some balls like the guys on TV. The first novice gripped his gorgeous Callaway club with his Nike glove and lunged at the ball with all his might. The ball did not move. His friend attacked the ball with similar gusto, hitting it a hundred yards perfectly straight. The only problem is that it was vertical. I tried my best to be quiet. After several more torturous swings, all with similar results, one turned to me and asked, "Okay, what am I doing wrong?"

"Everything," I winced. "First of all, neither one of you is smiling. You need to. If you don't laugh at golf, you'll never enjoy it. Laughter helps. And remember, golf is a simple game. All you have to do is get that little white thing into a four-inch hole in the ground 400 miles that way."

I told them three things. "First, line your feet up straight. Second, keep your head down when you swing. Forget about everything else and keep your eye on the ball. Third, swing your club straight back then bring it straight through."

"That's it?"

"For now it is. I want you to remember that golf is not about the clubs you swing, or the clothes you wear, or about trying to impress your colleagues. The key to playing this game well is to keep doing the right things over and over until they become part of your swing."

One of my favorite verses for golfers is found in Hebrews 12:12-13. "So take a new grip with your tired hands and stand firm on your shaky legs. Mark out a straight path for your feet. Then those who follow you, though they are weak and lame, will not stumble and fall but will become strong."

Just as there are fundamentals in golf, so there are fundamentals in our spiritual lives. First we must keep our eyes focused on Christ. He alone gives us life and hope. By taking a firm grip on His Word, the Bible, we gain strength and the wisdom to walk a straight path. When we keep our head down in prayer, we encounter one of the greatest resources available to those who follow the Master. Regular time with Him gives us all the tools we need to follow through on every task He gives us. Those who develop worthwhile habits excel in golf and life.

To the best of my knowledge, my two college friends have not yet made it on the tour. But both are now enjoying regular rounds of golf.

As for the Golf Channel guy, he just called to tell me about a brand-new 9-wood guaranteed to shave three strokes off his game. Now it will take him *12* holes to break a hundred.

—⁓—

I will study your commandments and reflect on your ways. I will delight in your principles and not forget your word.

PSALM 119:15

Question of the Day: What is one fundamental of my faith I tend to forget when life gets cluttered?

Tip of the Day: Golf instructor Andra Kirkaldy said, "I am thoroughly convinced that thousands of golfers today have had their game hopelessly ruined by neglecting simple first principles." So go easy. Let the clubhead go back and forward like a pendulum. Practice small swings first. Go little to big. Grip the club tightly only when throwing it.

5

Fore Is Short for Forgiveness

Never break your putter and your driver in
the same round or you're dead.
Tommy Bolt

My son almost killed a friend of mine the other day. It's not something we talk about a lot around town. In fact, only a handful of people know about it.

Until now.

The first tee box beckons us with promises of hope and the opportunity to start again. It's something my son and I have been thinking about the past few days.

We were standing on the first hole of our little course with grand visions of the round ahead. Jeffrey had a new driver with a head like a waffle iron. Carefully placing a brand-new ball on a brand-new tee, he stood back, took a few perfect practice swings, and then smacked his first shot. Hard.

To say he hooked the shot is like saying the Sahara Desert has sand in it.

My friend Lyndon Earl had been enjoying his round until then. He was standing on the second green less than a hundred yards away, lining up a long putt and thinking pleasant thoughts, when he heard two guys yelling "Fore!" at roughly the same decibel level as a teenager's stereo.

Unfortunately, he barely had time to blink before the ball struck him hard on the thigh. Lyndon thought he was dead. I thought he was dead. Running toward him as fast as we can run in golf shoes, both Jeffrey and I were wondering if we should call an ambulance or a hearse.

Thank God, Lyndon was okay.

Later that day, Jeffrey and I showed up at his house with a card and a gift. Lyndon limped to the door and smiled at us as we stood there apologizing for the eleventeenth time.

"No problem," said Lyndon. "I'm a welder. I'm used to incoming objects."

He was kind enough to show us the bruise, of course. The size of a small beach ball, it was not pretty. In fact, it looked like a giant discolored prune. With dimples. Surprisingly, its owner offered us a bigger gift than we could ever offer him: the gift of forgiveness.

I talked with a former Buddhist once, asking him what he saw in Christ that he never saw in Buddha. He didn't even pause to think about it. "Forgiveness for my sin," he said.

Recently, I watched another story of forgiveness unfold during the prestigious British Open. Though Ian Woosnam was ranked number one in 1991, travels in his own jet, and has a putting green at his home, he had been on a downhill slide according to the media. But here he was atop the leader board, tied on the last day of the tournament with four other golfers. At only five feet, four inches tall, Woosnam was poised to stand tall on the winner's podium.

After nearly acing a hole, he found himself leading the final round. Bending over to tee his ball up, he turned to caddie Miles Byrne for a club.

Instead, he got the shock of his golfing life.

"You're going to go ballistic," Byrne told him.

"Why?" asked Woosnam.

"We've got two drivers in the bag."

Woosnam knew immediately what it meant. He had 13 other clubs. With two drivers, that made 15. Only 14 are allowed. Woosnam had to call a two-stroke penalty on himself. A penalty that would knock him out of the lead.

"At that moment, I felt like I had been kicked in the teeth," Woosnam later said.

When the day was over, he had fallen four strokes short of the winning score posted by David Duvall and was left wondering what might have been had one of the worst gaffs in major championship history had not occurred.

But the response of the two men is the real story. What would you expect from the caddy? Some finger-pointing at least. A list of excuses for sure. Surely Miles Byrne could find someone or something to blame for his mistake. Instead Byrne said, "You want me to stand here and make excuses? There is no excuse. The buck stops at me. My fault, two-shot penalty, end of story." How unusual to read a story in the papers of someone accepting responsibility for his actions.

And what about Woosnam? How loudly would the

Welshman yell when he fired Byrne, the caddy who may have cost him his last chance at a major championship? Surely no one on earth would blame him.

The *Irish Examiner* printed his response: "With a super-human show of forgiveness Woosnam did not murder Byrne."

"It's the biggest mistake he will make in his life," said Woosnam. "He won't do it again. He's a good caddie. He will have a severe talking to when I get in, but I'm not going to sack him."

As the two walked together down the fairway to the eighteenth green, the crowd rose to its feet, giving them a standing ovation. Failure and remorse. Repentance and forgiveness. I think I've read that story somewhere before.

—∿—

If you forgive those who sin against you, your heavenly Father will forgive you. But if you refuse to forgive others, your Father will not forgive your sins.
MATTHEW 6:14-15

Question of the Day: Whom do I need to forgive this week?

Tip of the Day: Pros like Ben Hogan and Byron Nelson talk about "pronating" and a "lateral shift." Harvey Penick calls it the "magic move." Here it is: When you start your downswing, shift your weight to your left foot while bringing your right elbow back down to your body. Practice it over and over and over. Except during meals and board meetings.

6

The Real Golfer

*I found out that all the important lessons
of life are contained in the three rules for
achieving a perfect golf swing: (1) Keep
your head down. (2) Follow through. (3) Be
born with money.*

P.J. O'Rourke

One of my favorite PGA players is without a doubt Phil
Mickelson. During an interview with late-night talk-show host
Conan O'Brien, Phil was asked what he would do to celebrate
winning the Masters. Would he be drinking a lot? Mickelson
said, "I'll spend time with my family. I don't need alcohol to
help me have a good time."

Mickelson is known as Lefty because...well, because he
plays golf left-handed. But did you know that Lefty serves
tennis balls right-handed? He writes right-handed. He holds

a fork with his right hand. In fact, the only thing Lefty grabs with his left hand first is a golf club. The reason is most interesting. When he was one and a half years old, Phil learned the game by standing across from his father and watching him swing. His father plays right-handed. Mickelson simply mirrored his father's swing.

In Ephesians 5 we are told to do exactly that. "Be imitators of God…as dearly loved children." Or as The Message puts it, "Watch what God does, and then you do it, like children who learn proper behavior from their parents."

And what does this proper behavior look like? Paul goes on to list a number of things, which I think can be broken down into the acronym G-O-L-F-E-R.

Grateful

A foursome of seniors hit the course one day with waning enthusiasm. "These hills are getting steeper as the years go by," one complained. "These fairways are longer," griped another. "The sand traps seem to be bigger than I remember them," whined the third. But the oldest and wisest of the four said, "Just be thankful we're still on the right side of the grass!" Paul warns us what to refrain from while we're on this side of the grass, and twice he invites us to give thanks to God (5:4,20). Are you a grateful golfer?

Openhanded

Ephesians 4:28 instructs us to "give generously to others in need." Recently the *Wall Street Journal* published a story about Liz Perle McKenna, a New York writer who threw a most unusual fortieth birthday party. Instead of asking guests to bring presents, she had them come to her home and take one thing with them when they left. She said, "What I own doesn't say who I am anymore." But what we give says a lot about us. Those who mirror Christ mirror a God who, "though he was very rich, yet for your sakes he became poor, so that by his poverty he could make you rich" (2 Corinthians 8:9). If we own something we can't give away, maybe it owns us. I was thinking about throwing such a birthday party, and the first thing that came to mind that I'd miss is a Callaway 9-wood. I must ask myself, am I a grabber or a giver?

Loving

When asked about meeting his opponents before a round of golf, PGA star Seve Ballesteros said, "I look into their eyes, shake their hand, pat their back, and wish them luck, but I am thinking, 'I am going to bury you.'" Perhaps you can relate. I know I can. But Paul is challenging us to choose a higher road: "Live a life filled with love for others," he says, "following the example of Christ, who loved you and gave himself as a sacrifice to take away your sins" (Ephesians 5:2).

Forgiving

A popular word used in golf advertisements today is *forgiving*. Small wonder that those who are used to following a thick rule book that doesn't include the word *mulligan* are drawn to that word. I just saw an ad for a Ping 2-iron boasting that it is "designed for maximum forgiveness." Aren't you glad God extended maximum forgiveness to us? In return we are to forgive one another "just as God through Christ has forgiven you" (Ephesians 4:32).

Encouraging

My son Jeffrey loves the game of golf because of the kind words of two men we were paired with in a tournament when Jeffrey was a kid. They praised his putts and marveled when he mashed a drive past 50 yards. I sometimes wonder if he'd be enjoying the game today were it not for Jim and Neil. Paul would have applauded Jeffrey's swings too. He encourages us to "get rid of all bitterness, rage, anger, harsh words, and slander… instead, be kind to each other" (Ephesians 4:31-32).

Rejoicing

Those who reflect Christ demonstrate joy. They know that the fruit of the spirit is not prunes. One of my friends is Martha Bolton, who wrote many of Bob Hope's jokes for years. He used them at golf tournaments involving U.S. presidents and other celebrities. My favorite is this one directed at Gerald Ford, who once accidentally hit a tennis partner with a serve: "At least he can't cheat on his scorecard because all you have to do is look back down the fairway and count the wounded." Martha knows the secret to joy. It comes from mirroring the Master and living all of life in sight of eternity.

You may remember Gatorade's commercial "Be Like Mike." If I recall correctly, it went something like this: "Sometimes I dream that he is me, you've got to see that's how I dream to be, I dream I move, I dream I groove like Mike…I wanna be like Mike."

Thankfully, God has something a little better in mind for us—that we would be real golfers. That we would be like Christ.

—〰—

Exercise daily in God—no spiritual flabbiness, please! Workouts in the gymnasium are useful, but a disciplined life in God is far more so, making you fit both today and forever.

1 TIMOTHY 4:7 MSG

Question of the Day: Which mark of a "real golfer" do I most need to work on?

Tip of the Day: Chip the ball when the lie is poor, the green is hard, and you've had a bad day. Pitch the ball when the lie is good, the green is soft, and all is well with the world. If you don't know the difference between a chip and a pitch, just hit the thing.

7

Simple Pleasures

*The place of the father in the
modern suburban family is a very small one,
particularly if he plays golf.*
BERTRAND RUSSELL

*Daddy, I know you didn't win, but like I
always say, first is worst and second is best.*
FIVE-YEAR-OLD DAUGHTER OF
LEN MATTIACE, AFTER HE LOST A PLAYOFF
TO MIKE WEIR AT THE 2003 MASTERS

Back in the early days of my employment at Prairie Bible College, actual cash was scarce. Accepting this job for money was a little like going to Iceland for the weather. In fact, the banker asked my wife one day if she would like to open a joint account with me. She said no. She'd prefer to open one with someone who had money. But through the years God has never let us down. He constantly surprised us with His goodness and His unexpected gifts. Although a round of golf at Pebble Beach was out of the question, God surrounded me with resourceful people. Like my neighbor Vance.

Vance always managed to build something from nothing. Bookshelves from salvaged junk. Handcrafted porch swings from discarded maple. Waterslides out of plastic for the amusement of our small children. One day I watched him build a huge jungle gym out of power poles he had found somewhere. I still don't know where he got them. But I do remember our power being a little intermittent that week.

Upon finishing the towering structure, Vance informed me he had enough pieces of wood left over to build an elevated green and that he would be constructing it in the vacant field that lay behind the row of houses on our street. "Be up by nine," he said, his eyes sparkling in anticipation. "I think we can get you on."

Thus was born the Airport Golf and Country Club, so named for the abandoned airplane hanger that dominated the south end of all 18 fairways.

Early the next morning I lazed in bed as Vance mowed the entire field with his new red lawnmower. He raised the blade high enough to avoid any rocks we'd thrown out from our gardens, which bordered the course. Our fairways made the rough at Pine Valley look like worn Astroturf.

Now you know... One of the most ridiculous aces ever recorded was hit in 1959 at Cotswold Golf Club in England by John Remington. His 5-iron shot ricocheted off a drainage pipe in the rough, skittered across the grass toward a greenside bunker, bounced off a rake, rolled onto the green, glanced off the ball of his playing partner, and plopped into the hole. The act has never been repeated.

The Airport Golf and Country Club was unique in that it had 18 fairways but only one green. The holes were determined by varying the location of the tee boxes, and every few holes we adjusted the soup can in the massive elevated sand green. The hangar would serve a dual purpose, providing shade from the hot sun so we could practice on the green—or brown, as I called it—and serving as a solid backstop to keep our errant drives from decapitating pedestrians on the sidewalk that ran along the ninth and eighteenth holes.

As I lay in bed listening to Vance circle past, I smiled and cracked my knuckles in expectancy.

During the day Vance and I golfed a little, but mostly we manicured the course, throwing rocks from the fairways and pulling weeds from the green. In the late afternoon we began the Airport Classic.

Nearby our wives were tending hot dogs over a fire pit full of glowing embers. Amid five half-dead pine trees called Sherwood Forest, our children were shooting each other with imaginary guns, and all was well with the world.

We started on the first tee, smack dab in the center of my backyard. "Replace your divots," my wife reminded us. And we did of course.

The first hole was a sharp dogleg left, and the smaller children were asked to vacate the swing set before we took aim. The second hole was a straight shot from Vance's backyard, a lob wedge over the raspberries and across the garden. Number three required a sand wedge from the neighbor's doggy minefield, the splitting of two tall spruce trees, and the clearing of a towering thicket of dense lilac bushes. To this day it is one of the most challenging holes I've ever encountered.

After three holes we broke for juicy hot dogs and entertaining stories from the children of their adventures in
Sherwood Forest. After supper they climbed the trees to watch
as we completed our spirited game, which culminated in the
final challenge of number 18. The last hole was the longest,
as the tee lay beyond Sherwood and across the road on Larry
McClanahan's front lawn. From there you had to clear Larry's
car in his driveway, then the road, then the five-tree forest and
a grove of maple trees. Larry watched from the window with
his fingers crossed.

Hitting and sticking the sand green off the tee was considered to be a hole-in-one. But we never accomplished it. Some
days I wish I could go back and try again.

A few years ago the ancient hanger was removed in the
name of Progress and for safety reasons, I suppose. The fairways have long since grown over. I imagine the yards are in
better shape now. They have fewer divots, to be sure.

Since that time I've had the opportunity to golf some magnificent courses from Hawaii to Bismark, but few memories
are as sweet as those of simpler times at the Airport Classic.
Time spent with a good friend while our wives tended the hot-
dogs at the fire pit and our children peeked out of Sherwood
to cheer when we banked a good rebound off the hanger wall.
Isn't God good?

—⁓—

*A pretentious, showy life is an empty life; a plain and
simple life is a full life.*
PROVERBS 13:7 MSG

Question of the Day: What is one practical thing I could do to simplify my life?

Tip of the Day: When you're playing for score, go with the club that works. I once birdied a par 5 using only a 7-iron. When putting with a 7-iron, it is often necessary to block out the scorn and derision of your playing partners.

8

While I Was Watching

My dad's love was conditional. It was based on my golf performance. My advice is to let your kids know they are loved regardless of how they play.

BEVERLY KLASS, WHO WAS THRUST INTO COMPETING PROFESSIONALLY ON THE LPGA TOUR WHEN SHE WAS TEN

The only golf instructor I ever had was my father. He used to tell me, "Swing hard, Son, just in case you ever hit it." Though Dad rarely golfed with us, he purchased the first clubs I ever used and allowed me to smack golf balls from our backyard into a farmer's field each spring (until the field was planted). Every book I have written has had my father's fingerprints on it in some small way. With exhortation or generous laughter, he encouraged me that writing books is a lot like golf. Make each shot count. Finish what you start.

I was following his advice, trying to meet the deadline on the book you are holding, when the phone call came: "Your father may not make it through the night. You'd better come." It was June 30.

And so we canceled a tee time, gathered the grandchildren, and sped to the hospital, where Dad had been flat on his back for a few days with Alzheimer's-related pneumonia. The next morning, as the sun rose on his face, my father passed away.

From time to time during the next few weeks, I sat at the computer trying to write, throwing words in the air and hoping they'd land somewhere sensible. But how do you summarize 83 glorious years? How do you write a tribute to one who modeled the unconditional love Beverly Klass longed for? (See the quote above.)

Finally, I decided to write a letter Home.

Dear Dad,

We laid you to rest on a Wednesday under the wide Alberta sky. I was hoping for a stray rain cloud to disguise my tears, but I wasn't alone in that department. Saying goodbye to one you've admired since you were knee high to a tricycle isn't easy. But one who taught you to golf? One who loved you enough to say so? It is positively heartbreaking. Teenagers don't hang out

Now you know... Arnold Palmer said his father, Deacon, always knew his son's future lay in golf. "He'd say, 'Be tough, boy. Play your own game,'" recalls Palmer. "If you start listening to other people when you're out there, I have a job for you pushing a lawnmower back here at Latrobe Country Club.'"

in cemeteries much, but your grandkids refused to leave on Wednesday.

The night before you crossed the River Jordan, they crowded your bed and sang the hymns you loved to hear. "Amazing Grace." "How Great Thou Art." Twice you took my daughter's hand and tried to raise it to your lips. When at last you succeeded in kissing it, she began to weep from sadness and joy and the delight of another memory she'd carry for life.

And that's what you were about, Dad. Memories. When I was a lad, I loved to sneak up on you and watch what you were doing when you didn't know I was there. That's when you became my hero, I suppose.

When you thought no one was watching I saw you hit a golf ball in our backyard. I saw you slice it off a tree and hold your breath while it whacked your car, leaving a tiny dent. I held my breath, knowing that for the first time in my life I would hear my minister father swear. Instead you danced around using strong language like, "Oh shoot!" Then you snickered.

If anyone had reason to cuss, you did. Your mother died when you were two, leaving you roaming the streets of your hometown alone while your father toiled in a furniture factory. Raised by crazy uncles in a home where the unspeakable was commonplace, you graduated from the school of hard knocks before you entered first grade. But you never shouldered a backpack of grudges. Instead, you warmed our cold winters by telling stories of a childhood I found enviable, one jammed with fistfights and sports and loaded rifles. You told those stories with a twinkle too. That twinkle was a way of life for you.

When you thought no one was watching I learned how

to treat a lady. I learned to honor her and open doors for her and when to tip my hat. I learned that we're toast without the women, so put them first in line at potlucks. I learned to let them stroll on the inside of the sidewalk so when we're hit by an oncoming truck they'll still be around to care for the kids. I learned never to complain if par for us is 198 yards and only 112 for them.

When you thought no one was watching I learned what was worth chasing. You avoided the deceptive staircase promising success, investing in memories instead. You never owned a new car but scrounged to buy tent trailers and golf clubs for family vacations. You blew money on ice cream so we'd stay at the table longer. You bought flowers for my mother and gifts for my children. Watching your life, I learned that simplicity is the opposite of simplemindedness, that those who win the rat race are still rats. Going through your dresser last night, I found your glasses, heart pills, and a reading lamp. I suspect you're doing fine without them. In a file marked "Will" you'd misplaced a note Mom gave you listing your attributes. She made you sound like Father Teresa. "On time for work. A gentleman. Filled with integrity. Wholesome in speech. Loves family. Loves God." I guess it was filed correctly.

It's the best inheritance a child could hope for.

When you thought no one was watching I learned how to bring God's Word to life. Hours before you passed away I had you to myself. You were struggling to breathe, and my singing didn't help, so I told you I loved you and thanked you for being a good dad. Then I opened the same old King James Bible I watched you read when I was a boy. You'd underlined some glorious verses in Revelation 21, and I read to you nice and loud about that place where our tears will be wiped dry and our question marks straightened into exclamation points. By the time I reached the promise that your name is written in the grandest scorecard of them all, the Lamb's Book of Life, you were sound asleep. Friday morning you simply stopped breathing. No more tears. No more Alzheimer's. Home free.

You'll be glad to know your granddaughter Elena braided your comb-over the way she'd done it a hundred times before. We sat by your bedside as your daughter Ruth said, "Do you suppose he's saved?" And we laughed way too loud—from the deep assurance that you're with Jesus.

Some kind soul said, "I'm sorry you lost your dad." I smiled and replied, "Thank you, but I haven't lost him. I know exactly where he is."

When you thought no one was watching I learned how to die. With relationships intact, with nothing left unsaid.

Four of your five children were there. When we went to tell Mom of your passing, Tim asked, "Do you know why we're here?" "Money?" said your wife of 62 years. You'd have been proud of her.

She held your hand then, clinging to the last of your warmth. For the longest time she didn't say anything, just stared out the window. I asked what she was thinking, and she smiled. "I'd like to take one more stroll in the grass with him." Wouldn't we all? When they came to take you away, she simply said, "Thanks for all the years, sweetheart."

I'd like to thank you too.

Thanks for taking me golfing and teaching me to fish.

Thanks for majoring on the majors. And for a thousand time-less memories. Thanks for modeling how to finish the race, how to keep the faith.

Most of all, thanks for giving me a glimpse of what God looks like.

Each time I drive to our golf course I pass your grave. Each time I will give thanks for your life. Tonight I'll lay flowers there, and past the tears I'll determine to keep that twinkle alive. To live so the preacher won't have to lie at my funeral—as you cheer me on, all the way Home.

—⁓—

The mouth of the righteous man utters wisdom, and his tongue speaks what is just. The law of his God is in his heart; his feet do not slip.
PROVERBS 37:30-31 NIV

Question of the Day: How can I live so the preacher won't have to lie at my funeral?

Tip of the Day: Make sure you have a balanced follow-through. Your weight should be shifted to your front foot, and your elbows will end up in front of your body. The follow-through will reflect what went on before. The same is true in life. The legacy of those whose word is good as gold, who model integrity and how to finish the race, will last forever.

9

The Most Important Shot

You can make a lot of money in this game.
Just ask my ex-wives. Both of them are so
rich that neither of their husbands work.
LEE TREVINO

Golf is a lot like my spiritual life. It's full of just abouts and what-ifs. It's crammed with oopses and uh-ohs and the occasional "Ugh!" The game affords me an unvarnished glimpse of my soul, and to be honest, I rarely like what I see. At such times I know there will be no golf in heaven. I have proof from the Bible. Revelation 21:4 says there will be no more crying there.

Of course there are times of complete victory. Times when the fairways are unreasonably wide and the cup seems more like a basketball hoop. But these times are short-lived.

Lately my golf game has been a lot like the Old Testament. An unending series of adventures, detours, betrayals, and tragedies, sometimes interrupted by a miracle. Landing my ball on the green has been as easy as landing a Boeing in my backyard. The hole seems barely large enough to support the flagstick. I hit certain clubs and then check to make sure the number on the head is right. Could someone have played a cruel joke?

A few weeks back my son Stephen was on a practice range and misjudged the distance to the mat. He has what I call a pretzel swing—winding himself up then letting go—and when he swung his 5-iron, the head hit the plastic mat so hard that he bent it into a 2-and-a-half-iron. Amazingly, it has become the best club in his bag. He pulls it out when golfing with friends and proceeds to send the ball screaming 240 yards straight down the fairway. The friends want to know what club it was. "A 5-iron," says Stephen, humbly, showing them the number. "I held up on it—didn't want to kill the thing."

But that's not my story these days. Two hundred and forty yards is possible with a 1-wood. Down a steep hill. With a stiff breeze.

A reporter once asked a pro golfer about the secret to his success.

"Two words," said the golfer.

"And what are they, sir?"

"Good shots."

"And how do you make good shots?"

"One word."

"And what is that, sir?"

"Experience."

"And how do you get experience?"

"Two words."

"And what are they, sir?"

"Bad shots."

As surely as we learn to walk by stumbling, we learn to golf by duffing.

Here is my secret to better golf. It is a big part of the reason I've managed to shave a dozen strokes from my handicap in the last few years. It is simply this: I began to carry a second ball. I did not use the ball to cheat with—I swear. I did not cut a hole in my pocket and slip the ball down my pant leg in the rough. I used it to correct what I had just done. When I shanked or sliced or duffed and no one was in front of me or waiting behind me, I would drop another ball and try to correct what I had just done.

Better golf is about learning from our mistakes and pressing on. I guess it's about failing forward.

Have you ever wondered what is the most important shot in golf? Is it the drive? The putt? The chip?

Now you know... David Toms held a six-shot lead on the final hole at the 2003 Wachovia Championship in Charlotte, North Carolina, and then proceeded to make it interesting. Crisscrossing the fairway he finally made it to the green on his fourth shot and then four-putted from 47 feet for a quadruple bogey. His nearest challenger, Robert Gamez, bogeyed, so Toms won anyway.

Each of these is vital, but the most important shot in golf is undoubtedly the next one.

Just last week, on a short 340-yard par 4, I took out my 1-wood and spanked the ball 250 yards...straight up. Despite my coaching, the ball did exactly what I told it not to: It came down 40 yards in front of me. So I shared some thoughts with my golfing buddies about these long tees and my lagging eyesight, thoughts they didn't really want to hear. Then I took out a 3-wood and surprised myself by landing the ball just shy of the green, and then I went up and in for par.

In this case, the most important shot was not my pitiful drive. It was the next shot.

I'm not recommending that you duff your first shot on purpose. I'm not saying the tee shot is unimportant. But once it's done you can't improve on it. You can only learn from it.

Some of the dearest saints I know have left me shaking my head. If I were in their shoes, I would have packed it in long ago. One man I golfed with has lost his house to a fire, his daughter to a tragic car accident, and his wife to an affair. He could be hounded by regret and bitterness. He could give way to the sin of comparison. Instead, he takes the next shot. His secret is one of tireless perseverance, graced by thanksgiving. The only reason he looks in the rearview mirror is to find out how to move ahead.

Perhaps the key to golf is the key to life. "Forgetting what is behind...I press on toward the goal to win the prize for which God has called me heavenward in Christ Jesus" (Philippians 3:13 NIV).

—⁂—

In your love you kept me from the pit of destruction;
you have put all my sins behind your back.
ISAIAH 38:17 NIV

Question of the Day: What failure in my life has prepared me to succeed?

Tip of the Day: Uphill lies make you pull the ball. So shorten your uphill leg and straighten the other, keeping your hips level. On a downhill lie, do the opposite. Straighten your downhill leg and flex the uphill leg. Practice this shot. Better yet, practice staying away from hills.

10

Drive-By Golfers

*I've had a good day when
I don't fall out of the cart.*
BUDDY HACKETT

*If you want to beat somebody on the
golf course, just get him mad.*
DAVE WILLIAMS

We were on the first tee, two friends and I, when he roared up in his own custom-made cart. "May I join you?" he asked, pleasantly enough. Of course he could. We introduced ourselves to him, but he wouldn't volunteer his name. His eyes were shifty, never landing on us for long. And before long we found out why he was golfing alone.

He rarely spoke, only grunted. And when he did, ugly things spilled forth. He murmured about the foul weather, he muttered about my swing. And when he missed a shot himself or duffed, topped, sliced, or hooked, he would smack his club into the turf and say things that made us want to throw some soap in the ball washer and run him through it.

Not only was his vocabulary limited, he insisted on teeing off from a different tee box, causing us to wait each time. Though we hooted and hollered and clapped when he sank a 14-foot putt, not once did he acknowledge one of our good shots (yes, we had a few). He grumbled and groused his way from shot to shot, and at the end of the round, he stomped off the green without acknowledging our presence.

One of the men I was golfing with was a new believer in Christ, a muscular man who had worked for years on the oil rigs and could outcuss the most articulate cusser. He knew exactly what to do with our new golfing buddy. As we walked the eighth fairway together, he told me what he was going to do. He would nudge the man's cart into neutral and then push it into the creek—preferably with its driver behind the wheel.

I said, "Nah, you can't."

"Why?" he grinned. "Give me one solid reason."

"You're a believer now."

He smiled, "Sometimes it's no fun being a Christian."

And sometimes it's no fun dealing with people who drive us crazy.

One gorgeous spring day, my brother-in-law and I played golf at the Coyote Creek Golf Course in beautiful Redmond, Washington, where we found ourselves paired with Dan, a delightful guy who was as excited to golf as we were. Dan shot par on the first hole and celebrated with a beer. On the second hole he didn't have anything to celebrate, but that didn't stop him. By the third hole he was on his fourth beer. And by hole number five, his demeanor had radically changed. Pointing his clubs at geese, he yelled, "Die, you ugly duck…" He told the birds things they didn't know about themselves, things about their history and their future. And then he began to tell them about us! Mercifully, he quit and wandered into the woods, never to be seen by us again. He may still be out there.

On and off the golf course we find them, obnoxious people who test every ounce of our patience. They whine, they control. They hand us free tickets for an all-inclusive two-week guilt trip.

While climbing aboard a flight recently I was chastised by a lady one row in front of me for accidentally touching her sweater when I put my luggage in the overhead compartment. Sitting down, I listened to a fascinating conversation beside me.

"Do you smoke?" one man asked, sniffing the air.

"Yes," replied his seatmate.

"I thought so," the man said. "You stink. Smoking's dumb."

I should have checked the calendar. Maybe it was International Day of the Rude Person.

Perhaps you've bumped into someone today who drove you bananas. What was your response?

Any missionary will tell you the number one problem on the mission field is not theology. It involves interpersonal problems. I've been in countries where you need two things to be a good missionary: A good sense of humor and no sense of smell. Laughter certainly helps, doesn't it? But here are a few other ideas for dealing with problem people on and off the links.

1. Learn from them.

The impatient golfer behind can remind us how not to

golf. The driver who cuts us off in traffic provides an excellent opportunity to resolve never to cut someone else off. The
boss who chews us out shows us how not to treat others if ever
we are in charge. So send them each a thank-you note. Well,
maybe not. But don't let such opportunities be wasted. Learn
from them.

2. Pray for them.

Listen to the Master's revolutionary advice in Luke 6:27-
28 (NIV): "Love your enemies, do good to those who hate you,
bless those who curse you, pray for those who mistreat you."

3. Show them grace.

Let's face it: A little bit of The Jerk resides in us all. Each of
us needs piles of pardon and plenty of patience. So wage peace
by extending to others the grace we would want extended to
us. When we think of it, what have we done to deserve God's
favor? Does He love only the loveable? Jesus taught us to "Do for
others what you would like them to do for you" (Matthew 7:12).
Some of the softest people I know have a gruff exterior. When
I faced an acquaintance of mine with the fact that I felt insulted
whenever I played golf with him, he was shocked. And changed.
What I discovered beneath his abrasive sandpaper personality
was a guy who needed acceptance, patience, and forgiveness.

Days after playing golf with Dan, the beer-guzzling duck
hunter, I found a fascinating story in the paper. Not far from
the golf course, state wildlife agents found a black bear passed
out by a lake. Clues were scattered nearby—dozens of empty
beer cans. The bear apparently got into campers' coolers
(Dan's perhaps) and used his claws and teeth to puncture the
cans. And not just any cans—he appeared to favor one brand

over another. "He drank the Rainier and wouldn't drink the Busch beer," said Fish and Wildlife enforcement Sergeant Bill Heinck. "The bear did try one can of Busch but ignored the rest." The beast then consumed 36 cans of Rainier.

Wildlife officials shot the bear for its gluttony. No, I'm kidding.

Agents used a large humane trap to capture it for relocation, baiting the trap with doughnuts, honey, and two open cans of beer.

You already know what kind.

I wonder sometimes why we don't extend as much compassion and grace to humans as we do to an inebriated bear.

—~~—

Go easy on those who hesitate in the faith. Go after those who take the wrong way. Be tender with sinners, but not soft on sin.

JUDE 22-23 MSG

Question of the Day: Whom did this chapter bring to mind? Where do I go from here?

Tip of the Day: When you putt, take one or two practice strokes to judge the distance. Then keep your head perfectly still and imitate that stroke. Inside six feet, keep your eyes on the ground where the ball was sitting even after stroking it. You may want to listen for the ball to hit the cup. If someone yells "Fore!" temporarily disregard this advice.

11

Golfing with My Wife

Ruth and I are happily incompatible.
BILLY GRAHAM, ON HIS 62-YEAR MARRIAGE

Golf is like marriage. It tests our devotion and our ability to remember the good when things are less than pleasing.
JOHN SCHLEE, FORMER PGA TOUR PLAYER

Marriage counselors claim there are three activities that can destroy a marriage as quickly as anything. Building a house. Wallpapering. And going golfing together. Ramona and I have done all three. Building the house wasn't such a big deal. Wallpapering was a cinch. But golfing? That's another matter.

We have only played golf six or seven times as a couple, but when we do, one of my great weaknesses becomes glaringly evident. I am impatient. I know this surprises you. It has been a surprise to my wife too.

Golf can bring out the worst in me and rarely more so than when I golf with my spouse. I have golfed for 35 years, but I still cannot understand how someone who has golfed for 35 minutes can't hit a drive past 50 yards. And so I begin to coach her. I start with the stance and the grip and the swing. In less than 38 seconds I give her a lesson that most amateurs would murder for.

Then she steps up to the ball and kills another gopher.

Now I know that patience means biting my tongue when I feel like wagging it. That patience is a virtue, that it is a fruit of the Spirit. But I sometimes wish this patience would hurry up and get here.

Ramona and I have had our share of arguments on the course, and one of us is to blame. I believe that arguing with your spouse is a lot like trying to blow out a light bulb. Especially when you're wrong.

Recently I laced a perfect tee shot straight down the fairway and turned to Ramona as if to say, "See, Darling, that's how it's done." But she wasn't paying attention. If you can believe it, she was watching a great blue heron lift off in flight. Imagine the nerve.

I said something so dumb then that I surprised even myself: "Come on, we're here to golf, not to enjoy ourselves."

Now you know... At a club tournament on San Francisco's Lake Merced Golf Course, amateur Charles Greenstone Jr. cracked an errant shot over the green, past the entrance road, and up a walk to the clubhouse kitchen, where a cook holding a bowl containing two eggs opened the door just in time for the bouncing ball to make a perfect splat. A bowl-in-one. And that's no yolk.

Thankfully both of us began to laugh. It's something we've learned to do during 23 years of marriage. And quite frankly, if we weren't able to laugh, we'd probably be in a home somewhere weaving baskets together.

During the writing of this book, we have faced a series of hardships that has caused any troubles on the golf course to pale into insignificance.

In July we buried my wife's brother Dennis two days after my father's funeral. Dennis had suffered for more than two decades from a deadly genetic disorder called Huntington's, a disease that has invaded Ramona's family. Two of her sisters also have it, and their children are all at risk.

This morning we received an e-mail from a nephew informing us that Ramona's sister Miriam has been hospitalized for good.

During the past eight months her deterioration has accelerated to the point where she sometimes doesn't recognize her own children. After seeing a recent CT scan, doctors remarked that they couldn't believe Miriam could still walk and carry on a conversation. Due to pure determination and will, she has been able to keep doing some of the things that are important to her. But after ten years of patiently caring for her night and day, Miriam's husband, Jim, is left with no other alternative than to put her trustingly into the care of others.

Jim and Miriam's attitude in the face of overwhelming obstacles has been a testimony of God's grace from day one. "It doesn't seem to bother her that she is not at home anymore," says her son David. "As long as she knows where her bed is, that there will be food for breakfast (especially for all the others), and that she gets her Frappuccino." He put on a huge smile after these words.

In the midst of this valley, Jim and Miriam have shown their children and hundreds of others that one of the keys to a joy-filled life is allowing adversity to bring us together, not tear us apart. Talk about patience and perseverance. These two are shining examples.

At a family reunion a few years ago, Jim and I attempted to play golf together. The weather was awful. A horizontal rain was stabbing us from the north, and dark clouds threatened us with lightning bolts. We ended up putting for a few minutes on the practice green before quickly retreating from the storm.

How thankful I am that Jim did not retreat from the most major storm of his life. How thankful I am for the example of this saint of a man—one of my heroes.

I was thinking about Miriam and Jim the last time I played golf with my wife. Thoughts of them changed everything. I would be a fool not to be grateful for my wife's health. And for each and every day we have together. I would be a fool not to take a little longer to give instructions. I even say "good shot" a little more often now. In fact, I have said this about 112 times on 9 holes. And I've noticed that she's enjoying the game a little more now.

We were talking about what we'd like to do together if God allows us to grow old together. And one of the things we mentioned is golf. It will sure beat hanging around the house. Especially if she wants to hang wallpaper.

—◊—

And mark that you do this with humility and discipline—not in fits and starts, but steadily, pouring yourselves out for each other in acts of love, alert at noticing differences and quick at mending fences.

EPHESIANS 4:2-3 MSG

Put on then, as God's chosen ones, holy and beloved, compassion, kindness, lowliness, meekness, and patience.

COLOSSIANS 3:12 RSV

Question of the Day: How can I be more like Jim when the storms of life come?

Tip of the Day: The absolute best golf tip I can offer a young person is this: Find a great partner and marry well like I did. God bless you, Ramona. Thank you, Lord.

12

Wolf

*If you pick up a golfer and hold him
close to your ear, like a conch shell,
and listen, you will hear an alibi.*
FRED BECK

*Forget your opponents;
always play against par.*
SAM SNEAD

Good friends not only know what you want on your birthday, they deliver it. And so it was that three of mine showed up to whisk me from work for a round of golf on the forty-fourth anniversary of the day I came into this world. I was bald that day. I'm going bald again. I had no teeth that day. I won't say any more.

On the way to the course we decided on a game called Wolf.

The rules of Wolf are simple. Before teeing off, you establish an order that will roll over through the entire round. It

69

matters not how you choose the order. It can be determined by height, age, shoe size, waist size, or hair length, should you still have some.

The first player in the rotation tees off, followed by players two, three, and four. On hole number two, the second player in the rotation has honors and so on. The order then repeats itself until 18 holes have been played, and the loser has to jump in the creek or whatever punishment has been preordained for him. The player teeing off first is the wolf. As the wolf watches the others shoot, he has the option of picking one of them as a partner on the hole. Sadly, there is no waiting to see how all the players fare before choosing. The wolf must announce his intentions before the next player tees off. If the wolf passes on number two, he can tag player three but only before the last player hits. The same goes for the third player. If the wolf decides none of the shots are to his liking, he may go it alone and play against the other three.

To win a hole, the wolf and his partner must combine to make a lower score than the opposing team. A tie is a wash. A wolf playing alone must beat all others by a stroke and wins triple or loses triple. Because the seventeenth and eighteenth holes are left over after four turns of the rotation, the player in last place is generally given the courtesy of teeing off first and being the wolf on the final two holes.

The invoking of this last rule became necessary after our birthday round.

On the first hole, Ron and I were paired together, but we lost to James and Vance. On the 185-yard par 3 second hole, we found ourselves together again but in danger of falling behind two strokes. Apparently Ron had hit the creek with his first shot—though we couldn't tell—so he hit a provisional ball onto the green for his third shot. I was still quite confident he could locate his first shot, and sure enough, as he rummaged through the tall grass, he found it and then chopped it onto the green. Thanks to his amazing recovery, we won the hole.

On hole number four I decided to go Lone Wolf, hoping to pull ahead of the pack, and that's when Ron, who enjoys losing about as much as Napoleon, began whispering comments to the others before each of my strokes. "When did he rip his pants?" he'd whisper, just loud enough for the snickers to start. Since everything is funnier when it's not supposed to be, the snickering picked up. Then Ron dialed my cell phone from his.

As you might suspect, I lost the hole but gained a burning desire to beat the pants off my opponents.

The four of us jockeyed for position, and with two holes to go Ron was two enviable points ahead of the field. Never mind that he hadn't shot the greatest round of his life—that's one of the beautiful things about Wolf. He who picks well wins big. And Ron the Whisperer was winning. I tried a few whispers of my own, but his concentration was impeccable.

With one hole to go, Ron was beating the rest of us by one misery stroke, and since it was his turn to choose, he chose me. That's when he discovered the one glaring flaw in the game of Wolf: The leader's partner can throw the game. And so it was that I carefully lined up a two-foot putt to ensure that Ron won the match. I threw grass in the air. I walked around the ball twice, measuring the green for undulation.

Then I smacked that two-foot putt 50 feet across the green and into the murky creek.

Later, as we lounged around Vance's living room eating

cake with far too much frosting, we recounted the round for our wives, laughing until they shook their heads in disgust.

But Ron had saved the best till last.

Seems that ball on the second tee was still in the creek. "I cheated," he admitted. "I had another ball in my pocket. I dropped it. I hit it on the green." Confession was good for his soul. Ron's wife Karen was shocked. As was I. I'm sure you are too.

I'm still not completely over it.

Ron had been out of contention the entire time.

I was going to come up with some wonderful spiritual application from this story. Something about picking the right friends and vengeance being the Lord's. But all I can think of is the fact that I could have won that birthday game had I not chosen to go Lone Wolf.

So it is in life.

For the past 15 years I have met on a regular basis with five men who hold me accountable. Ron, Vance, and James are three of them. You may have noticed that this book is dedicated to the Circle of Six. Eternity will show what their friendship has meant to me.

Our course has a few lone golfers. They play at their own pace and barely keep ahead of foursomes. You'll find one of them throwing grass in the air on perfectly calm days. Licking a finger and holding it in the breeze—on the green. He moves through our 9-hole course like a deer through an anaconda.

I understand the desire to play solo golf. Solo golf gives you a tiny glimpse of how badly you could beat all the guys in the clubhouse if you could play them when they weren't watching. I have always been my best when no one was looking. I hit my longest drives and sink six-foot putts with my eyes crossed. I'm as predictable as a Holiday Inn. But life isn't lived solo.

When Jesus walked the earth, He could have done so alone. But He chose 12 men as companions. The old preacher Charles Spurgeon said, "Friendship is one of the sweetest joys of life. Many might have failed beneath the bitterness of their trial had they not found a friend."

If you don't mind, I'd like to tell you one more story in the next chapter about my friend Ron.

—〰—

Let us consider how to stir up one another to love and good works, not neglecting to meet together, as is the habit of some, but encouraging one another.
HEBREWS 10:24–25 RSV

Question of the Day: Do I tend to play Lone Wolf? What would help me be more accountable?

Tip of the Day: C.S. Lewis once wrote that "friendship is the greatest of all worldly goods. Certainly to me it is the chief happiness of life. If I had to give a piece of advice to a young man about a place to live, I think I should say, 'Sacrifice almost everything to live where you can be near your friends.'"

13

Heart of the Matter

You need a fantastic memory to remember the great shots and a very short memory to forget the bad ones.
MAC O'GRADY

Recently I turned 44. My wife threw a little cheesecake party, invited some friends, and handed me birthday cards. I loved the first one. It said, "Birthdays are like golf. The higher the score, the more we're tempted to lie about it." The rest of the cards had to do with aging too. My friends thought the cards were the funniest things they'd seen in weeks. They passed them around and snickered and snorted. They laughed until they could barely hang on to their walkers.

The worst thing about turning 44 is not the wrinkles or the walkers. It is the fact that I cannot read things without holding them in another area code. If evolution were true, our arms would stretch as we age, allowing us to hold documents where we can read them. I believe the overhead projector was invented by middle-aged church-going guys who could no longer read their hymnals. They needed things projected on the far wall.

This ailment is embarrassing in airports. I have to set the ticket on the floor to tell which gate I am departing from. People look at me funny. Little kids snicker. I try to trip them with my cane.

I was ambling around a golf store recently and found exactly what I wanted from the in-store flyer. A kind young lady asked if I needed help, so I pointed at a picture of a dozen golf balls and said, "I'd like four of these."

"Wow," she said, "where would you like them delivered?"

"No thanks," I responded, "I'll carry them myself."

She laughed and looked at my biceps. "Power carts are pretty heavy," she said.

If I have one consolation, it is the fact that I am aging in a close circle of golfing buddies. Ron Nickel is one of them. Sometimes Ron joins me when I travel to speak. On one such trip he told me about a visit to the doctor. Ten years ago a physician probed and prodded and listened to Ron's heart. Then he sat down and shook his head. "Your cholesterol count is higher than the price of oil," he said. Ron was not surprised. Like me, he loves few things more than a juicy steak followed by a triple-decker cappuccino cheesecake smothered in chocolate sauce. Ask Ron if he would like a little ice cream and he'll say no. He'd like *a lot* of ice cream. But the doctor ordered him to change his eating habits, to get more exercise, or he would be staring down the barrel of a heart attack ten years down the road.

But Ron is only three years older than me. When he visits the old folks' home, he's young. Invincible. Besides, he nears a donut shop and his car switches to autopilot.

On a Tuesday, Ron and I had a small disagreement. I won't give you too many details, but we fought over something so paltry, it's hardly worth mentioning. Okay, it was a golf case—one you would use when traveling. Never mind why, but there was a simple mix-up in payment rendered, and before we knew what had happened, the silence between us threatened to turn the issue into something larger. I was mad. I hung up on him. And determined not to talk to him again until the year 2399.

I knew all the Bible verses about forgiveness. I knew what happens when you carry a grudge, but it sure felt good for a few days.

On Thursday Ron called to ask me out for coffee. "Will you pay?" I ventured. "You bet," he laughed.

And so we found ourselves in a quiet coffee shop, talking of our families and of golf and the busyness of middle age. Then we got serious. "My father-in-law died a few weeks ago of a massive heart attack," Ron reminded me. "He spent the last hour of his life on a hospital bed, talking on his cell phone, repairing relationships. It's quite a lesson to keep short accounts." I was squeezing a creamer and choking back tears. "I'm sorry, Ron," I said. He had tears too.

Three days passed. I was holding the fridge door open, looking for—well, for donuts—when the phone call came. Ron had just had a heart attack.

Shocked, our family gathered in the living room to pray for God's intervention. God heard those prayers before we asked them.

If you're wondering where to have a heart attack, location is everything. Just ask Ron. Thankfully he wasn't on the golf course, but he was a short putt from an ambulance—an ambulance that was completely staffed. Just for good measure, a doctor "happened" to be walking by—one who is no stranger to such things.

My golfing friends and I have watched Ron's recovery with interest. And it's not just because we were hoping he'd willed us his 7-wood that he can hit 180 yards. We care about this guy. Ron's wife and children care even more. They laugh at his change of diet, but they couldn't be happier to have him alive. Me too. Ron's near-death has brought some changes to my life. I'm a little more careful about what I eat, for one thing. And what I say yes to. I've decided to find out who's gonna cry at my funeral and to hang out with them. This morning I pasted this to my computer monitor: "Since everything around is going to melt away, what holy, godly lives you should be living!" (2 Peter 3:11).

I suppose real life does not begin until we face our own mortality, until we shift our complete confidence from ourselves, or our health, or our finances—to God.

While I've been writing this chapter, the phone rang twice, I kid you not. First my wife informed me that the doctor would like to see me for something they call a physical. "I'd rather see a dentist or a financial planner," I told her, but she wouldn't budge. "I've given birth to three children," she said, "you'll do fine."

A minute later Ron Nickel called. Looks like it's my turn to pay for a bran muffin and some sugarless creamless decaf coffee.

Then we'll be heading out to the golf course.

With my eyesight problems, I'll have to hold the scorecard with my feet.

—⁓—

If you call God your Father, live your time as tempo-rary residents on earth.
1 PETER 1:17 GW

Question of the Day: If I knew I had one week to live, what's the first thing I would do?

Tip of the Day: There's a guy on our course who moves so slowly he looks like he's sweeping land mines. Pam Barnett said, "To help your concentra-tion, don't take too much time." Endless preparation on the tee equals too many conflicting thoughts. After a brief warm-up swing, remember one or two things you must do to hit it straight and swing away. Don't think of excuses until after you hit the ball.

14

My Green Jacket

*Golf is not a game of great shots. It's a game
of the most misses. The people who win
make the smallest mistakes.*

GENE LITTLER, FORMER PGA TOUR PLAYER

Most tournaments I am privileged to attend offer prizes ranging from hats that make me look like Elmer Fudd to sleeves of Top Flite balls to a brand-new Volkswagon Jetta. I am pleased to tell you that I have won two of these three prizes.

My favorite hole at any given tournament has always been the short par 3 with the car or the sign that tantalizes me with how much I will win if only I can shoot straight.

I have had interesting times of prayer while standing on those par 3s.

Gazing longingly at the Jeep Cherokee glistening in the midday sun, or the trip for 14 to Tahiti, I make deals with God.

I say, "Lord, first of all, help me not to miss the ball like

I did on the last tee. And, if You don't mind, please help this little white thing drop into the cup. I know it's presumptuous of me, but when I win, I promise I will sell the Jeep and give you…um…11 percent. Or no, make that 12."

Then I stare down the flagstick 180 yards away and look down at my spindly arms and revise my prayer. "Lord, how about 20 percent? No, we'll split it 50/50. I promise."

Statistically speaking, I know I have more chances of hitting a striped kangaroo with a spitwad than I do of hitting a hole in one, but still I pray. I've heard the odds are 1 in 13,000, but still I hope.

My friend Vance accompanied me to a tournament recently in Kelowna, British Columbia, at a meticulously groomed course called The Bear—designed by the Golden Bear himself, Jack Nicklaus. As we stood on a par 3 that offered $10,000 for an ace, I began to think of the people I could help with that money, and I prayed hard. The hole was the 190-yard number 14, which for me requires a long iron shot, a stiff breeze, and a miracle not unlike the parting of the Red Sea. The shot must carry McIver Lake and find a green that slopes front to back, making it virtually impossible to stick it by the hole.

In 35 years of golfing I had yet to hit a hole in one. I had come within a foot or two. I'd bounced shots onto the green from carts, trees, water hazards, and ball washers. But I had never experienced the joy of watching from the tee box as the ball teetered on the edge then rattled around the cup.

Not yet.

I think I purposely avoid hitting aces because my home course has an annoying custom written by someone who had never hit a hole in one: The acer buys drinks. In fact, you buy them for everyone in the clubhouse, including people who drove out to the course when they heard what you did. To me, this is a little like celebrating Father's Day by bringing the family breakfast in bed.

Still I stepped up to the number 14 tee with gladness in my heart and a 4-iron in my hands. I cleaned the grooves in that club with a tee. I scrubbed a blade of grass from the ball. And I prayed. I prayed that God would erase my bad habits and cause a miracle to take place.

Then I took a swing.

My release was magnificent. My follow-through was enviable. The four of us watched in awe as the ball took off straight as an arrow. One of us tried not to act surprised. The ball accelerated as it rose, traversing the lake and continuing to climb. It descended beautifully as if radio controlled, honing in on the flagstick, causing my heart to leap with anticipation.

The lady who was there to witness any surprising events rose from her golf cart. The lady danced the polka for about two seconds, and I knew the ball was in the cup. She buried her face in her hands and I couldn't tell if it was from grief or glee.

I ran to the green, but there sat the ball.

It left its mark one foot in front of the pin and somehow rolled straight over the hole, coming to rest 18 awful inches behind the cup. I asked the dear lady if I didn't at least get something, you know, a consolation prize, maybe just $4000 or a hat. She said no. Close only counts in lawn darts.

"Come on, God," I said, as I tapped the stubborn ball into the hole. "Was it too much to ask?"

I'm sure you've never done this. I'm sure you don't need a reminder that God is not a vending machine. But sometimes I do.

I spoke that night on "The Divine Mulligan of Grace," but

before I did, I spied a warm green jacket on the auction table. It was leather sleeved with a classy golf insignia on the front. I needed a jacket, I really did. Unfortunately, I noticed that bids could start no lower than $100. Since my wife and I stick to a preordained budget and people were generous with their bids, I knew the jacket would never be mine.

I don't recall praying for some divine miracle, but afterward, as the organizers were thanking me, one of them brought me the green jacket and said, "Here, do you want this? It fell behind the table." I swear I did not push it off the table, but I gladly wrote them out a check for $100. Today that green jacket is a well-worn reminder that God has a good sense of humor and that He cares for our needs.

—◊◊◊—

Let us then approach the throne of grace with confidence, so that we may receive mercy and find grace to help us in our time of need.

HEBREWS 4:16 NIV

Question of the Day: Do I view God as a vending machine? What is one thing I want from Him? One thing I need?

Tip of the Day: To hit a fade, align your clubface to the target and then align your feet and shoulders so they are slightly open (facing to the left for right-handed golfers). Then swing normally. To top the ball, choke up on your club and lift your head.

15

True Strength

I prayed this morning, but I didn't pray
to win. I just thanked God to be alive.
You know, the everyday stuff. I've
never prayed to win a tournament.
I don't think that would be fair. Why
should He show partiality toward me?

REV. WALTER JESSUP, AFTER WINNING
HIS SECOND STRAIGHT CLERGYMAN'S
GOLF TOURNAMENT

You become stronger only when you
become weaker. When you surrender
your will to God, you discover the
resources to do what God requires.

ERWIN LUTZER

During the past few years the friend I've golfed with more
than any other is Mike Olver. Mike is younger than me, slightly
shorter, but monumentally stronger. In fact, Mike has muscles

in places where I don't even have places. He sometimes asks which club I am using just so he can fall over laughing. On a 150-yard par 3 with nothing but water between the tee box and the slippery green, Mike doesn't have to think about it. He grabs a pitching wedge. I point at some wildlife and pull out an 8-iron, hoping he doesn't notice. If I hit the pond, he asks, "What club were you using?"

"Sand wedge," I lie, and he just grins.

On most par 4s I use a Big Mama 1-wood. Mike outdrives me with a 3-wood. And sometimes a 4-iron. One of these days when he isn't looking I might just bend his clubs.

Mike runs the dining hall at the college where both of us work, and sometimes the golf course manager at our local links asks him to help run the clubhouse. As much as possible Mike says yes. Not long ago when the golf course staff held their annual party, Mike was there again. Checking people in. Taking phone calls. Flipping burgers. Listening to golf stories—a big grin all over his face.

There's something you should know. Mike takes nothing in return. No money, no rewards. He wouldn't want you to know about his generosity, but he is not writing this book. I asked him once why he does it. He said, "What do I need? I've got a car that runs, a wife who loves me, and a son to golf with."

His eyes get a little misty when he tells you this. You

Now you know... One of my favorite golfers is Briny Baird. Like other pros, he uses his golf bag to promote something. But not clubs or cars or corporations. Briny's bag features an important phone number, 1-800-THE-LOST, a help line for missing children. Baird also donates $100 for each birdie and $250 for each eagle he makes to the National Center for Missing and Exploited Children. Says Tiger Woods, "Being able to help people and give back—that's what golf is all about."

may wonder why at first. Until Mike tells you the following story.

One dark August day a friend of Mike's died of a massive heart attack in the prime of life. He had the build of an Olympic athlete. He was training for a triathlon with his brother. Mike and his wife were shocked. A few weeks after the funeral, the Olvers invited the widow and her eight- and ten-year-old over for dinner. Mike noticed her looking at his golf clubs. "My husband was going to take the kids golfing," she said, staring into the distance. "He didn't get around to it."

Mike was fighting tears.

"Would you do something?" she asked timidly. "Would you take them golfing with you sometime?"

You already know Mike's response. Of course he would. "Do they have clubs?" he asked.

"No," she responded. "But I'll look for some."

One night after Mike finished running things at the Three Hills Golf and Country Club, he came by the house to show me something. There was a glow coming off his face, and it wasn't a sunburn. Seems he'd been preparing to lock up the clubhouse, when the manager came over to thank him for filling in. Clearly touched by Mike's kindness, he said, "You know, you do this for us every year, but you won't take anything in return. Isn't there something we can do for you?"

"Maybe," said Mike.

All evening he'd had his eyes on two items in the corner of the pro shop. When he had a few moments he wandered over to examine them. They were two beautiful sets of Top Flite junior golf clubs. A driver, a putter, and all the irons, shrink-wrapped in matching black and red bags, complete with shoulder straps and kick stands.

"Could you give me a deal on those clubs?" Mike grinned.

It was the manager's turn to grin. "Take 'em," he said.

Mike's grin got wider. "You're kidding," he said.

But the manager wasn't.

Mike couldn't stop smiling and shaking his head as he told me this. "I'll get some balls and tees and surprise these kids," he told me. "And I'll try to get their mom some lessons so she can take them golfing too."

Mike is one of the strongest men I know. I've played hockey against him, and you can't move this guy from the front of the net without a crane. But true strength has little to do with the physical. True strength has more to do with gentleness and a servant's heart. James 1:27 says, "Pure and lasting religion in the sight of God our Father means that we must care for orphans and widows in their troubles, and refuse to let the world corrupt us."

Mike revved the engine and took off to tell his wife. I knew I'd never have the nerve to bend this guy's clubs.

—◦◦—

It is better to be patient than powerful; it is better to have self-control than to conquer a city.
PROVERBS 16:32

Question of the Day: What is one thing I could do this week that would show true strength?

Tip of the Day: Davis Love Jr. said, "When it's breezy, hit it easy." It's good advice. Remember the wind is blowing as hard at the others as it is at you. Change clubs to keep it low. Keep your balance. Take your time. One more thing: Keep your eye on your club. I hate throwing a club and having to ask my partners where it went.

16
Lost and Found

My greatest fear is that he'll die before I do.
What will I do with all this stuff?
—Sharon Mates, wife of Barry Mates, whose
golf ball collection includes 50,000 balls
from all over the world

One dear old duffer on our course has given up on golf altogether. Oh, he doesn't mind hitting a ball now and then, but if you're standing near the tee box when he swings, you'll notice that he purposely aims for the creek. And when the ball goes where he intended, he feigns disappointment.

"You go on ahead," he smiles, "I'll catch up later."

As he says this, he slides his ball retriever from his bag and slips over the edge of the bank where the shanked balls hide. Every other club in his bag has failed him, but not this one.

It is a sad thing to watch the hunter become a gatherer.

I asked him one day about the secret to finding lost golf

balls. It was like I asked a fisherman to show me his favorite fishing hole. He squinted at me suspiciously.

"I'm not gonna follow you in there," I assured him.

So he whispered some things. Top secret things.

"You drag your feet," he said, "like this. And you wear bigger shoes than you need. They cover more ground. I'd say 25 percent of all the balls I find are found with my feet. I used to bring a rake out here to pull them out of the creek, but the manager made me stop."

He seemed surprised I wasn't taking notes. Like he was giving away the Great Caramel Secret or the directions to Atlantis.

"When you golf, you gotta notice where people lose balls. You keep track. Then you go back later, after they're gone. I wear gloves and long pants. They plant thorns on purpose, you know. Stinging nettles. Poison oak. You can't be too careful," he said. "I don't bother with the creek much. It's too murky. I shuffle my feet along close to it, but I face away. I look up the bank, the opposite direction from where the balls came in."

"Did you ever fall in?"

It was like asking a fisherman if he'd ever hooked himself in the ear.

"Oh, yeah," he laughed, "many times. See this?" He rolled up his pant legs. His shoes were wet and mucky, his calves were laced with thorny scratches.

"Is it worth it?" I asked.

He wouldn't even dignify my question with a response. His eyes were darting now, but he couldn't stop himself. "I haven't bought a sleeve in 20 years."

"What's the craziest thing you've done to find balls?"

"Sometimes I lay right down in the grass," he confessed, his eyes far away now, remembering wistfully. "I roll around. I don't do it so much anymore though."

"Why's that?"

"Thorns," he said. "And arthritis."

"How many balls do you think you've found?"

He chuckled humbly, but I knew it was the one question he was dying for me to ask.

"Three thousand this summer. They're in my garage. Buckets of them."

"Did you find any with my name on them? You know, Callaway?"

He stopped chuckling.

"Those are mine," I said, "you should give 'em back."

I had one more question for him. "What's the strangest, most bizarre golf ball you've ever found?"

He had to think about that one, so he did. "I found one with a fish on it," he said. "I think it was someone's way of sharing the gospel. There were words on the other side. It said, 'I once was lost, but now I'm found.'"

—◊◊—

When I was a little boy, a picture hung on our wall. I shut my eyes tightly, and I can see it even now. It is of the Good Shepherd hugging a lost sheep tightly to his chest. Beneath it a verse of Scripture stands out, forever reminding me of the extraordinary lengths the Master has gone to redeem lost sheep like me: "For the Son of man has come to seek and to save what was lost" (Luke 19:10).

Though I cannot understand it, He somehow found me worth looking for. No price was too high for our redemption. He paid it with His life. No distance was too far for Him to travel. The Creator of the universe came to earth as a creature. He came to die that we might live with Him forever. He came because He would rather die than live without us.

What is left to us but to live thankful lives, passing God's grace along every day?

The dear old guy on our golf course would agree, I think. This morning when I arrived at work I found half a dozen golf balls on my desk. Each one had my name on it.

—⁓—

So then, dear friends, since you are looking forward to [heaven], make every effort to be found spotless, blameless and at peace with him.
            2 Peter 3:14 niv

Question of the Day: When I hear God would rather die than live without me, what should be my response?

Tip of the Day: Don't lay a club on the ground before lining up. I have left behind and permanently lost perfectly good clubs this way. Instead, take your stance and hold the clubshaft against your thighs. This will show you where you're aimed. Don't forget to hit the ball.

17

Clubhouse Christian

*I'd play every day if I could. It's cheaper
than a shrink and there are no telephones on
my golf cart.*
BRENT MUSBURGER

*You have made us for yourself, and our heart
is restless until it finds its rest in you.*
AUGUSTINE OF HIPPO

Did you know there are people out there who call themselves golf historians? It's amazing. They can talk circles around
you or me when it comes to golf. If you bump into a golf historian or find yourself golfing with one for a round, you may
discover fascinating things about this game. You may also feel
like smacking the historian with a putter.

I golfed with a man recently who knew absolutely everything there was to know about golf. I was amazed and duly impressed. He knew obscure matters of trivia. "Did you know that Sandra Day O'Connor is the only U.S. Supreme Court justice to have scored a hole-in-one?" he asked.

I didn't know this.

He knew precisely where to stand when someone else was putting out or teeing off. He knew to bring a towel to the green to clean his properly marked ball.

The trouble was he couldn't golf worth a hill of beans. His putts were short and crooked. So were his drives. Except when he missed the ball altogether.

Though his etiquette did not allow him to get upset with himself, he really should have. If I golfed like that consistently I would have the common decency to throw my clubs in the creek and quit the game. But not him. Sure, he would frown after sinking that all important sixth putt, he would shake his head after shanking his fourth approach shot, but there was little emotion. He would rather talk about those who play the game well than do so himself.

You've met him too, I'm sure. He's the guy who looks great in the clubhouse. He's the armchair golfer. Oh, he does well at computer golf. Hook him up to a mouse and he can hold his own. Hand him a joystick and he can beat you hands-down. But take him onto the golf course where it matters and he's lost. Hand him a club and stand back.

When I was a little younger and my forehead wasn't so high, I knew much about God. If they'd have held a tournament for Bible trivia games I'd have won the grand slam. I could quote Scripture. Recite all four stanzas of a hundred hymns. But there was one small problem. I didn't know the One I was singing about. Though I was privileged to grow up in a home where my parents taught and lived the Bible, it hadn't taken hold of me.

We used to have "sword drills" in Sunday School. We held a Bible over our heads like the Sword of Damocles. When the teacher yelled out a Bible verse, we would frantically flip the pages until some winner found it. Guess who usually won? That's right. I was proud of how many verses I could find about the sin of pride. I looked down on those who couldn't locate verses about the Pharisees.

One day I encountered a story in the Bible that confused me. It was of Mary and Martha, two friends of the Master. I don't think either of them golfed—the Greek doesn't even hint at it—but Martha was a generous soul, so it's possible. One day she invited Jesus and His disciples into her home for a meal. Now, I've fed six teenagers at a time. Imagine feeding 13 grown men. But to make matters worse, Martha's sister, Mary, didn't even help out with the roast. As Martha sliced potatoes, Mary sat at Jesus' feet, listening and learning. Finally, Martha had had enough. "Lord," she complained, "doesn't it seem unfair to you that my sister just sits here while I do all the work? Tell her to come and help me." Though John 11:5 tells us that Jesus loved Martha, He scolded her: "My dear Martha, you are so upset over all these details! There is really only one thing worth being concerned about. Mary has discovered it" (Luke 10:38-42).

And it hit me like someone yelled "Fore!" Like me, Martha

was consumed by the temporary, while Mary was hungry and thirsty for the eternal. Like me, Martha was missing the essential ingredient to a living and vibrant faith: the desire to sit at Jesus' feet.

I had spent years living exactly like the golf historian, talking about the Master without really knowing Him. Jesus' words to the Pharisees were directed to me: "These people honor me with their lips, but their hearts are far away" (Matthew 15:8).

When our first child was born, I was hit hard once again. As I looked into the eyes of my curly-haired son, I realized that in no time he would see me for what I was: a hardened hypocrite. I realized I'd been close to the church but far from God. I knew I'd been reading the Bible for information, not for formation.

I knelt by my bed that night and prayed a simple prayer: "God, make me real. I want my precious little boy to hunger and thirst after righteousness. And if he won't learn to from me, he's got two strikes against him already."

I trust you too have prayed that prayer.

For all of us will wander restlessly searching for meaning, purpose, and fulfillment until we discover that our thirst can only be slaked by knowing the Master.

I'd rather play golf than talk about it, wouldn't you?

I'd rather sink a hole in one than know what the odds are that it will happen.

Of far greater importance, I want to know Christ, to walk in His presence, to learn from him. In knowing the Master I have come to the stunning realization that He knows us and loves us too.

I consider everything a loss compared to the surpassing greatness of knowing Christ Jesus my Lord...I want to know Christ and the power of his resurrection and the fellowship of sharing in his sufferings, becoming like him in his death, and so, somehow, to attain to the resurrection from the dead.

PHILIPPIANS 3:8-11 NIV

Question of the Day: What is one practical step I can take to know Christ better?

Tip of the Day: There is great debate as to where you should place the ball before you swing. Most teachers advise you to hit it off your left heel. I've managed reasonably consistent golf by ignoring their advice. For a driver and 3-wood, place the ball off your left heel. But move the rest of your shots slowly back until your wedge is dead center. When you pull the ball from the bunker with a rake, do so off your right foot.

18

But I Love You More than Football

There is one thing in this world that is dumber than playing golf. That is watching someone else playing golf. What do you actually get to see? Thirty-seven guys in polyester slacks squinting at the sun. Doesn't that set your blood racing?

PETER ANDREWS

I met a lady by the name of Anna the other day. She asked me how it's possible for me to be a Christian and play golf. I had to scratch my head on that one. Finally I said, "It's not easy, but I try. Pray for me, would you?" I thought it was one of my more witty comments in a while, but I soon discovered she didn't think so. Anna scrunched her lips and furrowed her forehead. My words made her furious. Apologizing is something humorists learn to do, but after I did so I wondered aloud why she felt this way. Anna proceeded to smack me with three irrefutable reasons we golfaholics should relegate our clubs to a yard sale.

1. Golf is a selfish, addictive sport. Golf widows are a dime a dozen, she said. Few golfers play golf with their spouses, and even fewer *enjoy* playing golf with them.

2. Golf is expensive. If we took the money all the Christians spent on golf and put it in the offering plate, we could do away with fundraisers and possibly telemarketers. She had a point there.

3. Golf is a complete waste of time. As sports writer Bruce McCall wrote, "No game designed to be played with the aid of personal servants by right-handed men who can't even bring along their dogs can be entirely good for the soul." Anna said that we are to redeem the time, for the days are evil. We aren't to be walking around playing cow pasture pool—fiddling while Rome burns—when there are things to be done. The same is true of fishing, of course, but at least most guys come home with something you can eat after a weekend of it.

Put yourself in my FootJoys. What would you say?

The truth is, I couldn't agree more. Any golfer with a shred of integrity will admit that sports can be addictive, selfish pursuits. When former Los Angeles Dodgers manager Tommy Lasorda was accused by his wife of loving baseball more than he loved her, Tommy consoled

Now you know... *Golf Magazine* asked 500 golfers, "Who is it most important to fake a loss to on the golf course?" Seventy-five percent said they would never take a dive. Four percent said letting the boss win was vital, and the top category at 11 percent: letting the kids win.

her, "Yeah, but I love you more than football and basketball."

Who doesn't know someone whose priorities get
scrambled while staring down the barrel of the latest sporting
event? Someone who spends too much on the habit? One who
would sooner work on his slice than his marriage? Golf can be
all about *me*. My clubs. My score. My shot.

But surely selfishness existed long before the advent of the
putter. And if so, then the problem lies not with the game but
with us.

I read an article about a couple who had lived their lives in
Minneapolis, suffering through 57 long, cold winters. Tired
of block heaters in their cars and tuques on their heads, they
finally called it quits, retiring to Florida to golf year-round.
(I'm from the frozen north, so I smiled to think of such a prospect.) But six months later the couple's tune had changed. "We
played golf every day. That's why we came here," said the husband. "But after a few months I started thinking, there has
to be more to life than this. We won't be happy until we find
something useful to do. Something that will make a difference.
I want more out of life than just playing golf."

The couple remained in Florida, golfing occasionally but
finding true joy immersing themselves in volunteer work at a
nursing facility, living life on purpose.

Now, no one enjoys golf more than I do, but picture standing
before God one day and explaining what we did with the gifts
He gave us. Picture saying, "Well Lord...ahem...I did break
90!"

Surely there are few things more tragic than coming to the

finish line only to discover you were in the wrong race. What could be more tragic than a wasted life?

I asked Anna the real reason she couldn't stand the game, and her eyes lowered. She told me her first husband had chosen golf over their relationship, eventually leaving her for a girl he'd been playing golf with. She told me how the man she loved now had just confessed to her that he enjoyed the occasional round, and she was ready to run away from home.

I told her a little of my own story.

Back in the fall of 1994, I was writing books, editing a magazine, speaking across the country, nurturing a marriage, and raising three rambunctious children. Admirable pursuits, all of them. But it was part of my theology that only a tired Christian is a productive Christian. I remember telling someone that I would rather burn out than rust out.

And I fulfilled my own prophecy.

Flat on my back, finished and caput, I had a doctor advise me on some changes I needed to make. He told me that sleep is the poor man's treasure. He suggested I learn to laugh more and trust others with administration I had taken on. He said I must learn to rest. To punctuate that final point, another visitor, a man of God who'd served Him for years, leaned real close and gave me a most interesting assignment.

"You should take up golf again," he said.

What was I to do? I had no choice.

During the next few months, I discovered that a few hours a week spent strolling groomed fairways sure beat Valium. I found that Psalm 23 made more sense after a round of golf. Like David, I began to spend time beside still waters (lots and lots of time looking for my ball), allowing God to restore my soul.

In Matthew 11, Jesus extends a stirring invitation:

> Come to me, all you who are weary and burdened,
> and I will give you rest. Take my yoke upon you and
> learn from me, for I am gentle and humble in heart,
> and you will find rest for your souls. For my yoke
> is easy and my burden is light (Matthew 11:28-30
> NIV).

My own spiritual life had become a burden. There was no room for rest. It had everything to do with what I put into it. If I had to sum up my spiritual life with one word, it would have been *do*.

I began to see that a better word is *done*.

For me the golf course has become a quiet haven where I can thank God for all He has done for me. Oh sure, I sometimes feel more inclined to wrap my putter around a tree, but when I give thanks for the beauty of His creation, for the wonder of Christ's atoning death for me on the cross, everything changes. Even my game shows temporary signs of improvement.

You'll be pleased to know that Anna is a recent convert to golf. She wrote me to say that she has been golfing with her new husband. She says she hasn't laughed this much in years.

He says he hasn't either.

—☗—

*You have made known to me the path of life; you will
fill me with joy in your presence, with eternal plea-
sures at your right hand.*

PSALM 16:11 NIV

Question of the Day: Would you agree that failure is succeeding at something that doesn't matter? How can I resist accomplishing this?

Tip of the Day: The best club you'll ever own is a good attitude. Play one shot at a time. Start again on the next hole. If this doesn't work and you have hit more than 18 shots on the first hole or hit more than one person, ask the course marshal. Sometimes they'll let you start again.

19

The Perfect Club

If you think it's hard to meet new people,
try picking up the wrong golf ball.
JACK LEMMON

If we let culture happen to us,
we'll end up fat, addicted, broke,
with a houseful of junk and no time.
MARY PIPHER, PSYCHOLOGIST

Without a doubt, the happiest golfer I know is Jason Miller. A young father of two, Jason routinely shoots well past a hundred, and that's just on the fourth hole. The funny thing is, he does so with a grin. Perhaps the grinning comes from knowing he will have a few hours of unbroken stillness away from his toddlers and his job as a youth worker. But I think it may have more to do with the fact that Jason has learned to golf light.

Apart from the digital organizer he uses to keep score,

Jason keeps it simple. So simple that he doesn't even own a golf bag, preferring instead to clutch five clubs in one hand: a driver, a five-wood, two rusted mid-irons, and a warped putter. Jason's pockets bulge with golf balls, and if he runs out, he simply waves foursomes through and then strolls the edge of the creek, parting grass and talking out loud. "Come on home to Papa," he beckons.

Standard wear for Jason is shorts, a collared shirt, and golf sandals. At times he golfs in bare feet. Says he can feel the balls better in the creek that way.

Jason's unencumbered style gave me the bright idea of walking the course with a 6-iron and a putter the other day, something I did twice in a row, trying to figure out why I shoot roughly the same score as I do lugging the full set—which includes an umbrella, a ball catcher, and enough snacks to outfit a Boy Scout troop.

An old duffer on our course saw me carrying two clubs and wandered over to the ninth green. "Here's one you gotta try," he drawled. "It's the only club you'll ever need."

I examined the grip and then the head. It was a clever little gizmo, I had to admit. A spring-loaded screw on the toe allows you to adjust the clubface trajectory from a sand wedge all the way to a putter.

"Great idea," I said. "Mind if I give it a try?"

"Knock yourself out," he said.

And I almost did.

> **Now you know...**Shooting a first-round 82 at the 2003 Nordic Open in Copenhagen sparked an unusual reaction from Mark Roe. He bet friends that he could break par the following day using just six clubs. Wielding only a driver, putter, 3-iron, 6-iron, and sand and lob wedges, Roe fired a two-under 70. He won his bet. but still missed the cut.

On the driving range I discovered the club to be the single worst invention in golf since someone decided to shrink the cup to four inches.

During a round I told Jason about the invention, and he was almost ready to trade his digital organizer for one. And so, thinking I stood to make a healthy profit, I told him of some other golf inventions that had impressed me.

There's the Glow-in-the-Dark Golf Ball. At long last we don't need to pause for something as trivial as sleep—we can golf all night.

"My wife isn't eager to see me going during the day," he said. "She'd kill me if I went at night."

I mentioned the Swing Speed Radar, which measures the speed of your swing as the clubhead whizzes past. "It runs on three AA batteries," I said.

"Does it run when I hit it with a golf ball?" he asked.

I didn't think so.

I told him about the Digital Golf Scope for checking the exact yardage to the pin. And the Caddypatch—just stick it to the clubface and discover exactly where you're contacting the ball.

He wasn't impressed.

Nor was he excited about the Rangemaster Distance Meter (a gizmo you mount on the right wheel of your golf cart to measure every yard you cover) or the Visiball Lens (glasses with lenses to help you find lost golf balls).

"I've got an idea," he said. "Let's build the perfect club."

And so as we golfed, we brainstormed a little. The Perfect Club would have a tiny built-in weed whacker activated by a button on the grip. A shot in the rough? No problem. Simply flip the switch and clear away the offending grass.

A second button would engage a high-powered blower for those putts that won't drop. They say 80 percent of short putts don't go in. Now 100 percent do. Just press the button and blow the ball into the hole. There would be a reverse switch, of course, for those bunker shots. Hit a sand trap? Not a problem. The blower turns into a vacuum nozzle. Ideally, you wouldn't swing the club, you would just line the ball up directly in front of the face, and pull a trigger.

Of course, all this stuff made us think of more stuff, and before long Jason got a little more serious.

"My wife and I are hoping to head overseas sooner or later, so we're downsizing," he said as he cleaned a ball off on his pants and teed it up. "We had a garage sale last week, and I couldn't believe how good it felt to be rid of stuff."

Jason took another swipe at the ball and walked toward the creek. I shouldered my bag and trudged along beside him. "I went to my high school reunion this summer," he continued. "Forty people my age. All they seemed to talk about were the houses they were building or the stuff they owned."

I must admit that God has been dealing with me about my stuff. I wish He wouldn't. Quite frankly, I love just about every little golf gizmo I've seen. But when you see a friend mourn the life of his dear child, when you watch your father die, certain things matter, and none of them are things.

I was flying into a beautiful city, looking down, admiring the golf courses, and I thought to myself, *Can you believe how big the houses are down there? I mean, who said we need houses three times the size they were in the 1970s? We're building big empty boxes for empty people who advertisers have convinced need huge homes because they need more room for all their stuff. We've got clocks to shine the time on our ceiling in the middle of the night and cell phones that work underwater. What we all need is something the advertisers can't deliver: We need peace, we need purpose.*

Some would call this approach to life rather simple, but the people I have come to admire most are the Jasons who "golf light." Those who recognize things for what they are—goods to enhance life, not weigh us down.

And so, amid historically unprecedented affluence, those who would walk with the Master are wise to do so unencumbered. We can start by buying less and giving more.

I think I'll will my old golf clubs to my son. And tell him there won't be a big nest egg waiting to burden him down. In fact, the last check I write is going to be to the undertaker. And it's gonna bounce.

—∼∼—

We fix our eyes not on what is seen, but on what is unseen. For what is seen is temporary, but what is unseen is eternal.

2 CORINTHIANS 4:18 NIV

Question of the Day: Do I own anything that is not enhancing my life but is weighing me down?

Tip of the Day: To increase your distance off the tee, warm up and stretch before you play. For $20 you can buy exercise tubing and practice your swing with resistance. Don't bring tubing to the course. Try this instead: If you're right-handed, tuck your right hand beneath your left. Gently apply pressure from the back of your right hand against your left as you slowly pull your upper body into your backswing. Hold 15 seconds and repeat. Actually hitting the ball further will require a club.

20

How I Learned
I Was a Sinner

You're looking up. That's your problem.
GRAFFITI ON THE UNDERSIDE OF THE ROOF OF
CART 47 AT SEA SCAPE GOLF COURSE,
KITTY HAWK, NORTH CAROLINA

Nothing dissects a man in public
quite like golf.
BRENT MUSBERGER

I know of few places where we will encounter our true selves more often than the golf course.

I *heard* I was a sinner in Sunday school.

I *knew* I was a sinner on the golf course.

A friend of mine stopped by my office the other day. His face was tanned from a summer of golf, but there was a paleness about his cheekbones. His knuckles were sweating, and he was tugging on his tie like it was a noose.

"What's wrong?" I asked, "Is it the kids? The wife? Did you just back over a cat?"

"Worse," he responded, rubbing his bloodshot eyes. "I went to see a golf pro. He showed me my swing. I always thought my swing was pretty good," he moaned. "But the video looks like I'm killing chickens with a sledge hammer. The frustrating thing about my golf game is that no matter how bad I play I can still get worse. I understand why so many people drink after they play."

Like a man who beheld himself for the first time in a mirror, he was unprepared for what he saw.

I don't know about you, but I don't need a video to inform me of my bad habits on the course. I don't need a freeze-frame remote to make me aware of my own shortcomings when golfing.

I'm sorry if you're disappointed in me, but here are three deadly sins I must subdue each time I'm out there.

1. The craving to cheat

When I hook a ball into the woods and find it behind a tree, everything within me cries, "Kick it three feet, you idiot! Who's gonna know? No one's watching. They're looking for the results of their own incompetence. And while we're at it, don't you find it convenient that the greatest game on earth is also the easiest one to cheat at?"

At such moments I am reminded of Bobby Jones' immortal words at the 1925 U.S. Open. When asked why he called a penalty on himself when the ball moved as he addressed it, he responded, "There's only one way to play the game. You might as well praise a man for not robbing a bank as to praise him for playing by the rules."

The penalty ended up costing Jones the championship.

2. The blunder into blame

I am constantly employing my Excuse Meter on the golf course. While playing with three other golfers in a skins game (the skins were golf balls), a wicked wind suddenly came from nowhere while I stood on the tee box. It hurled my ball left to the right and then died as quickly as it began. When finally I found the ball buried deeply in a shoe mark in a cruel, damp, unraked bunker, a little voice within told me exactly what to do. You'll be impressed to know that I didn't listen to the voice, but I ended up with a double bogey. The only immediate reward I could see as my friends unzipped that pouch and clamored for a brand-new ball each was that my bag would be lighter.

3. The appetite for anger

Golf makes me mad. Perhaps you're not like this. Maybe you're one of those who greets each shot with inner applause and a gentle cry of thanksgiving. Not me. I do not curse the course, but I've been known to grow obscenely silent. Some simply quit. Others grow violent, taking it out on their equipment. Or they abuse tee boxes, putting greens, and helpless shrubs. One player I read about became so infuriated when he chunked a routine pitch into a trap that he bludgeoned his ankle with his wedge until he drew blood, threw his club into the trap, dove headlong in after it,

> **Now you know...**Mike Ditka, fiery former head coach of the Chicago Bears, grew so angry at missing a short putt one day that he snapped the putter around his neck. Although he was in pain, in true Ditka fashion, he went directly to a speaking engagement. "I was surprised that none of my best jokes were going over," he remembers. Until he realized how badly he was bleeding. The snapped putter caused a severe gash that required 30 stitches.

and proceeded to lie on his back scooping sand onto his body and yelling.

I believe that is a two-stroke penalty.

Of course anger is not funny. It is one letter short of "danger."

A pastor friend of mine was enjoying a peaceful round one Saturday on a course a few hours from our house. But the foursome ahead of him was not. They could be heard yelling and cursing. After an errant drive, one raised his driver above his head, smacking the earth with such force that the flawed shaft snapped in half, causing the bottom half to rebound end over end, embedding itself in the man's neck. By the time they arrived at the clubhouse it was too late. The man died on the course in his mid-thirties, leaving a wife and two children behind.

"Of the Seven Deadly Sins," writes Frederick Buechner, "anger is possibly the most fun. To lick your wounds, to smack your lips over grievances long past, to roll over your tongue the prospect of bitter confrontations still to come, to savor to the last toothsome morsel both the pain you are given and the pain you are giving back—in many ways it is a feast fit for a king. The chief drawback is that what you are wolfing down is yourself. The skeleton at the feast is you."

In the classic devotional *Streams in the Desert*, Mrs. Charles E. Cowman tells how her mother would meet with the Master for one hour immediately after breakfast each day, with startling results. "As I think of her life, and all it had to bear, I see the absolute triumph of Christian grace in the lovely ideal of a Christian lady. I never saw her temper disturbed; I never heard her speak one word of anger...or of idle gossip; I never observed in her any sign of a single sentiment unbecoming to a soul which had drunk of the river of the water of life, and which had fed upon manna in the barren wilderness."

Anger is not always sinful, of course. Sin angers God. But anger on the golf course is rarely righteous. In Colossians 3:8 (NIV) we are instructed to rid ourselves of "anger, rage, malice, slander, and filthy language." Imagine a golf course (or a movie!) without them!

Many of us give way to our temper as though it were useless to resist, as if we owed it to our clubs. Or our coworkers. Or our spouse and children. But resist it we must. Not that we might lower our scores, but that we might walk in the footsteps of our Master.

—⁘—

My dear brothers, take note of this: Everyone should be quick to listen, slow to speak and slow to become angry, for man's anger does not bring about the righteous life that God desires.

JAMES 1:19-20 NIV

Question of the Day: What is one thing that is helping me conquer anger, blame, or cheating?

Tip of the Day: In *Golf Digest*, Paul Runyan gave this advice: "Don't let the bad shots get to you. Don't let yourself become angry. The true scramblers are thick-skinned. And they always beat the whiners." An old Italian proverb says, "Anger can be an expensive luxury." So take a lesson from a rocket ship. Count down before blasting off.

21

Improving Your Serve

Reverse every natural instinct and do the opposite of what you are inclined to do, and you will probably come very close to having a perfect golf swing.
BEN HOGAN

We must remember throughout our lives that in God's sight there are no little people and no little places. Only one thing is important: to be consecrated persons in God's place for us, at each moment.
FRANCIS SCHAEFFER

Behind every great man is a greatly surprised woman. And behind every great golfer is someone who doesn't mind letting another get the credit. It is the caddy.

The caddy is usually not a bad golfer himself, but at some point he decided that if someone else is gonna look good, he'd better step off the stage and shine the spotlight. Ever wonder how the pros line their feet up so straight? It's often the caddy who has done so off camera and then stepped aside. Ever wonder how they know the yardage so precisely? Thank the caddy and his little black notebook.

According to those who study such things, French military cadets carried clubs for golfing royalty back in the 1600s. The English then borrowed the word, and *caddy* came to mean, "What? You said a 6-iron. I knew it was an 8."

A caddy is responsible to carry the bag, rake bunkers, clean clubs, replace divots, find errant shots, tend pins, find the golfer's ball, and say "nice shot" as often as possible. He also provides the golfer with yardage, points out course hazards, tells him what the wind is doing and when he needs a 7-iron instead of a putter. But according to Michael Hunter, grand caddy master of the Old Collier Golf Club in Naples, Florida, there is even more.

"People ask me, 'What's the difference between a good caddy and a great caddy?'" says Michael. "A great caddy is able to read personalities. He will see that one guy doesn't want him to say anything—he wants to focus just on golf today. Another fellow might want to talk, talk, talk. A great caddy makes the golfer comfortable. If a golfer hits a bad shot, he has to reassure him and get him to focus again. A great caddy is a sports psychologist; he's your investment adviser; he's the weatherman; he's everything rolled into one. He also needs to give personal attention. The caddy is there to do a lot of the thinking for the golfer, so that all the golfer has to do is swing the club. A good caddy takes strokes off your game."

Reading Michael's words, I can't help but notice that the

best caddy delights in another's success. In a word, the best caddies love to serve.

When I think of servants, I think of Doug Nichols, my friend and unwitting mentor.

Back in 1966, Doug joined an organization called Operation Mobilization for a year of ministry in France. While in London for training, he volunteered to work on a cleanup crew late one night in preparation for a conference that was to begin the next day. Around 12:30 AM, as Doug swept the front steps of a building, an older gentleman approached and asked if he was in the right place for the conference. Doug assured him he was. "The man had a small bag with him and was dressed very simply," recalls Doug. "I told him I would see if I could find him a place to sleep."

The place Doug found was the room where he had been sleeping on the floor with about 50 others. Laying some padding and a blanket on the floor, he handed the man a towel for a pillow. The stranger thanked Doug and began preparing for bed. Doug asked him if he had eaten. "No," the man said, "I've been traveling all day."

The two went together to the dining room, where Doug found Corn Flakes, milk, bread, butter, and jam. As they ate, the man expressed his gratitude and told how he and his wife had been working in Switzerland mainly with hippies and travelers.

Upon awaking the next morning, Doug discovered that the man he'd been sharing Corn Flakes with, the man he had accommodated on a cold, hard floor, was none other than the conference speaker, Dr. Francis Schaeffer, one of the most famous Christians of the past century. (His wonderful quote is on page 114.)

Doug smiles about it now. "I have since thought about this occasion many times," he says. "This gracious, kind, humble man of God sleeping on the floor with mission recruits! This was the kind of man I wanted to be."

Doug has hardly played a round of golf in his life, but he has learned how to caddy. One day you'll find him handing out food to squatters in a garbage dump in Manila. The next week he'll be in Zambia or Rwanda, holding a child, comforting those who are dying of AIDS.

Like the ideal caddy, both Francis Schaeffer and Doug Nichols learned what it means to live for others. They have obeyed the humble words of Paul in Philippians 2:3-4 (NIV): "Do nothing out of selfish ambition or vain conceit, but in humility consider others better than yourselves. Each of you should look not only to your own interests, but also to the interests of others."

I'm told that the recommended tip for a caddy is $25 above the cost of a round. Most St. Andrews caddies will charge you $50 plus a "suggested tip" of about 20 pounds. But the rewards for a true servant are out of this world.

—⚬⚬⚬—

And don't let anyone call you "Master," for there is only one master, the Messiah. The greatest among you must be a servant. But those who exalt themselves will be humbled, and those who humble themselves will be exalted.

MATTHEW 23:10-12

Question of the Day: Do I respond like a servant when I am treated like one?

Tip of the Day: Nutrition experts advise golfers to avoid caffeine and alcohol (both are diuretics and cause fluid loss) and to drink lots of water. If you're a serious golfer, avoid large amounts of food in the two hours leading up to your tee time. Instead, eat five or six small meals throughout the day and pack a bag lunch. If you're bringing a teenager, pack five or six bag lunches.

22

Perfecting Failure

I have a tip that can take five strokes off
anyone's game. It's called an eraser.
ARNOLD PALMER

Courage is going from failure to failure
without losing enthusiasm.
WINSTON CHURCHILL

One of my favorite moments in the movie *Bobby Jones: Stroke of Genius* comes when a man asks his Scottish caddy what he can possibly do to improve his game. The caddy deadpans, "Stop playing for two weeks. Then give it up altogether."

If we're honest, we've all felt like quitting, haven't we? In golf. In life.

That's why I love the story of the late golf-enthusiast Charles Schultz, the creator of *Peanuts*.

Early in life his friends called him Sparky, though he hated the nickname. Sparky failed every subject in eighth grade and still holds the school record for being the worst physics student in the school's history. In high school he flunked physics, Latin, algebra, and English. And he seemed to be flunking Relationships 101. If a classmate said hello outside of school, he was surprised. If a girl looked his way, he was shocked. Sparky never dated or even asked a girl out. He'd dealt with enough failure in his life—why risk being turned down again?

At the age of 15, however, he began to excel at golf. He became a caddy, eventually claiming a trophy as St. Paul, Minnesota's caddy champion. By 17 Sparky was a two-handicapper, building his game around a deadly accurate power fade off the tee. But one dreadful day Sparky's poor play cost his school golf team the championship.

Turning his attention to drawing cartoons, he found that no one seemed to share his enthusiasm for his characters. Even the school yearbook committee turned him down. After graduation, he sent the Walt Disney studios samples of his artwork. Once again he was rejected.

Sparky began to realize that in some weird sort of way, his life resembled a cartoon strip. He decided to tell his own story in cartoons—a childhood full of the misadventures of a little boy loser, a chronic underachiever. Of course, this cartoon character is now loved the world over as Charlie Brown.

Since golf was one of Schultz' passions, his characters were often shown on the links. In fact, Schroeder is named after a caddy friend.

In one of my favorite golf cartoons, Charlie Brown is talking to Snoopy. "Tournament golf can be very nervewracking," he tells the little dog. "Do you get nervous when you're on the first tee?" "I don't know," responds Snoopy, shaking violently, "I've never made it to the first tee."

I'm so glad Charles Schulz didn't just make it to the first tee. He kept teeing it up well into his seventies.

He often played twice a week, mostly at Oakmont Golf Club in Santa Rosa, California, one of five Sonoma County courses where he was an honorary member. A fixture at the AT&T Pebble Beach National Pro-Am, Schulz was always mindful of the rules and was called "a tough competitor" by *Golf Digest*. With an annual income estimated at $33 million, he was listed as one of *Forbes* magazine's best-paid entertainers. One weekend he flew in two foursomes for a game of golf at Pebble Beach. On the way home he reminded one of them that he been shorted 50 cents on a bet.

In interviews, he let it be known that the thoughts expressed in the strip reflected his own hopes, fears, and faith. Schultz grew up in a Lutheran home, joined the Church of God as an adult, and taught a Sunday school class. He regularly injected biblical ideas, quotes from the Bible, and theological values into his strip.

"Sparky was very honorable to the game," said longtime friend and Oakmont Director of Golf Dean James when Schultz passed away at the age of 77. *Golf Digest* called Schulz "Golf's good man."

In her book *Good Grief: The Story of Charles M. Schulz*, Rheta Grimsley Johnson wrote, "Rejection is his specialty, losing his area of expertise. He has spent a lifetime perfecting failure."

I cannot read of Charles Schultz without thinking of a host

of Bible characters who perfected failure. If anyone had the yips, Moses did. Yet God helped him face his fear and lead the Israelites out of captivity in Egypt. David was guilty of adultery and murder. Still he was called "a man after God's own heart." Jonah ran from God and ended up down in the mouth. God used him to turn the hearts of an entire city heavenward. Each one of these knew where to go with his failure. They all knew it isn't falling down that makes you a failure. It's claiming someone pushed you. They knew that failure doesn't come in the falling, it comes in not getting back up.

With God's help, your greatest achievement may be lying just beyond your greatest failure.

—⟋⟍—

For though a righteous man falls seven times, he rises again, but the wicked are brought down by calamity.
PROVERBS 24:16 NIV

Question of the Day: How has past failure prepared me for the future?

Tip of the Day: If you allow for a slice, you'll get one. Concentrate on what it takes to hit the ball squarely. Famed golf instructor Harvey Penick advises you to "pretend you are on a baseball field at home plate... aim your body slightly to the right of second base, but aim your clubface straight at the base. Then hit the ball over the shortstop. Use a 7-iron at first, then a 3-wood." Work on your slice until you can hook the ball.

23

The Yips

Over the years, I've studied the
habits of golfers. I know what to look for.
Watch their eyes. Fear shows up when
there is an enlargement of the pupils.
Big pupils lead to big scores.
SAM SNEAD

Am I afraid of high notes? Of course I am
afraid. What sane man is not?
LUCIANO PAVAROTTI

Frustrated golfers, disappointed duffers, take heart! Mayo Clinic scientists, who are undoubtedly struggling golf enthusiasts themselves, are chipping away at the mysterious root of the yips—those involuntary twitches of the hand or wrist that defeat putts, crush spirits, and cause people to twist their putters into pretzels.

A new study suggests that the yips are tied to a task-specific movement disorder, like writer's cramp or tennis elbow. Unfortunately, there's still no cure, but take heart, someone somewhere is working on it.

What exactly do the yips look like?

A friend of mine is deadly with a putter. He's as confident as Eric Clapton with a six-string. I envy the smooth pendulum motion. The squinty eyes. From 14 feet he beats me every time. But put him 18 inches from the hole and he's 50-50. Give him a short putt and the squinty eyes cloud over.

He had the yips.

The yips are a million-dollar industry. Belly putters promise hope. An assortment of expensive training aids guarantee a cure.

Ranked number five on *Golf Digest*'s list of America's 50 Greatest Teachers, Hank Haney can solve your slice. He can disentangle your drive. He can even patch your putts.

Haney believes that the yips—not fatigue, stress, or some mechanical swing problem—have sabotaged the careers of David Duval, Seve Ballesteros, and Ian Baker-Finch. There's no other explanation for the high scores these immensely talented golfers are posting, he says.

In 1998 after the first round of the Masters, Mark O'Meara went straight to the putting green after shooting a disastrous 74. Haney says it was the most discouraged he

> **Now you know...** According to a *Golf Magazine* survey, 17 percent of respondents have missed work by calling in sick to play golf. One percent admitted they played hooky ten or more days a year just to play golf. But 54 percent said they would never lie to play.

had seen him in 23 years of working together. Haney started in on the standard post-round pep talk filled with clichés—two over isn't so bad, there's plenty of time to get back into the tournament, you can do it, Mark. But O'Meara knew better. "How can everything be okay?" he asked. "I have the yips from two feet in. I literally cannot make a putt."

Haney knew all about the yips. They'd almost caused him to quit the game forever. But overcoming them had given him the knowledge of what to look for.

"Mark had his eyes aligned way to the right of his target," he remembers, "which caused him to aim to the right. His hands were subconsciously jerking through impact to try to yank the ball back to the left and toward the target."

Haney merely helped him get his eyes back on target.

On Friday O'Meara shot a 70 to make the cut. Gaining confidence, he began sinking putts, both long and short.

Of all the 1998 Masters highlights, one is shown on television more than any other. It is of Mark O'Meara calmly rolling in a 20-footer on the last hole. The birdie putt gave him a one-shot victory over David Duval and Fred Couples and became the greatest moment in Mark O'Meara's career, an incredible feat when you realize how far winning was from his mind that Thursday afternoon.

When I heard this story I began thinking of the people I know who are uniquely qualified to offer advice when we encounter the yips of life. If someone has ever attempted to comfort you with a cliché, you know what I mean. "Just hang in there, you'll be fine." "Keep praising God, Brother." "Hey, time heals all things." And we feel like smacking them. But when someone comes along who has walked where we walk, who has endured an earthquake, battled bankruptcy, or suffered sickness, we tend to turn our ear and listen.

For five years a woman struggled with depression brought on by seizures. Barely able to go an hour without one, she longed for hope. She knew God loved her, but where was He? She cried out to Him, but the doors of heaven seemed locked, the windows bolted. "I know He's there," she said, "but it's like He's a neighbor who keeps borrowing my stuff and not bringing it back. How can I trust Him?" She felt like King Hezekiah, of whom the Bible says, "God withdrew from Hezekiah in order to test him and to see what was really in his heart" (2 Chronicles 32:31).

Today those years are a distant memory as medication has treated the source of the woman's trouble. But through that season of hardship I began to see what was really in her heart. Those trials paved the road to helping others. Her story has been read or heard by millions through radio and the books I've written. Her remarkable faith has been a daily testimony to me. She is of course Ramona, my reluctant golfing partner and my wife of 23 years.

Second Corinthians 1:3-4 (NIV) calls God "the Father of compassion and the God of all comfort, who comforts us in all our troubles, so that we can comfort those in any trouble with the comfort we ourselves have received from God."

Let us find joy, purpose, and fulfillment by helping others get their eyes back on the target.

—ɯ—

Be strong. Take courage. Don't be intimidated. Don't give them a second thought because GOD, your God, is striding ahead of you. He's right there with you. He won't let you down; he won't leave you.

DEUTERONOMY 31:6 MSG

Question of the Day: Who do I know that is battling the yips? What can I do today to help?

Tip of the Day: Don't chop your chip. Follow all the way through. Grip close to the steel and make your backswing equal your follow-through. Use the club that will put the ball on the green the quickest and get it rolling to the hole. Near the green, 30- to 100-handicappers should putt whenever possible. If you're higher than that, throw the ball.

24

Too Old to Golf?

What's nice about our tour is you can't
remember your bad shots.
BOB BRUCE, ABOUT THE SENIOR TOUR

I still swing the way I used to, but when I
look up the ball is going in a different
direction.
LEE TREVINO, ON AGING

If you try to get on our course first thing most summer mornings, you'll discover the tee time you hoped for is likely booked. If you squint your way down the list of foursomes there in the clubhouse you'll find that most of the golfers are people who refused to give up on golf when their body started hollering at them to stop. I love their tenacity.

I spoke with one member of our club who told me the aging thing has him perplexed. "I swing exactly the (bad word) way

I did 20 years ago," he groaned. "But the (really bad word) ball doesn't go as far. I'm swinging just the same, but I'm pulling out a (even worse bad word) 3-wood where I used to hit a 7-iron." I asked him what he does with the problem, and he couldn't think of anything good to say, so he inserted other words instead.

For the most part, however, older guys are a joy to golf with.

One Saturday afternoon my son Jeffrey and I had the pleasure of playing golf with two gentlemen, John and Earl, both of whom qualified for the seniors' restaurant discount 25 years ago. I noticed some things immediately. For one thing, they weren't as eager as I was to impress anyone. I'm not sure the exact age at which you stop thinking you'll make it on the PGA tour, but they had long surpassed it. Don't get me wrong, they still wanted to learn. In fact, John was trying to improve his putting stance, Earl said he needed to "come through" on his drives a little more. I found out later that Earl was a two-handicapper in his prime, but those days were long gone.

Both of these gentlemen had swings forged by decades of ailments. They brought their clubs back to the level of their belt loops and then swatted the ball as if they were chasing a cat with a broom. But not once did we look for their golf balls. My son and I hunted for ours, to be sure, but never theirs.

During that game I discovered I was slowing my

Now you know... While playing competitively, Jack Nicklaus has always carried three pennies in his pocket for marking purposes. Why three? "Years ago, an incident made me think that if I carried just one penny and lost it, I'd be without a ball marker. If I carried two, lost one, and a fellow competitor needed one, I'd again be without a marker. So it's three pennies for me."

swing down a little. I didn't try to kill the ball like I do when I'm golfing with my son's friends. I relaxed a little. I listened to stories of what things were like just after Noah got off the Ark. I even took a peek into their golf bags. Earl had fewer clubs than I carry. No three irons. No five irons, for that matter. Lots of old fairway woods. John said he never carried more than three balls. But I noticed he had two different types of ball retrievers. I didn't have the nerve to ask him why.

They were generous with compliments and stingy with complaints. They were short on criticism and long on laughter. They took an active interest in our lives and great delight when my son drove a ball 300 yards. Maybe they've learned that in the grand scheme of things golf doesn't matter so much. There are more important scores to be recorded.

I don't know about you, but I love the thought of a game that allows you to play until you drop. Like John and Earl, I'd like to be active in life long after the "Best before" date on my body. And more importantly, I'd like to be making a difference in the lives of others long into old age. Encouraging people, like these two encouraged my son. Still learning, still growing.

Since that round of golf, I've been asking myself an important question: At what age are we too old to grow? Too old to learn?

My mother, who is 81, is still reading voraciously. I had a letter from a 91-year-old last week saying that God had been speaking to her through something I had written. She said she'd been slack in her prayer life, that she needed to revive her love for Scripture. Ashamed, I wrote her back, telling her that God had spoken to me just as loudly through her letter.

Though I don't suspect she golfs, I told her about some older people I admire. Folks who demonstrate that the twilight years of life can be productive ones:

Leo Tolstoy learned to ride a bicycle at 67. At 82, he wrote *I Cannot Be Silent.*

At the age of 72, Greg Norman's mother, Toini Norman, was the reigning women's champion at Pelican Waters Golf Club in Caloundra, Australia. She aced the par 3 fourteenth hole at the course her famous son designed.

Thomas Edison was 84 when he produced the telephone.

At 90, Eamonn de Valera served as president of Ireland.

At 94, Leopold Stokowski signed a six-year recording contract.

At 100, Grandma Moses was still painting pictures.

Teiichi Igarashi celebrated his one hundredth birthday by climbing to the 12,395-foot high summit of Mount Fuji.

Arthur Thompson of British Columbia, Canada, shot his age on the Uplands Golf Club in Victoria—a course I have driven past but have yet to play. He was 103.

At well past 90, James "Clyde" Dameron was the reigning champ of the Senior Olympics in Southeastern Virginia. He was born the year Albert Einstein developed his special theory of relativity and William Taylor patented the dimple-pattern for golf balls. James shot his age twice when he was 75. He's done it so many times since, he stopped counting at 400.

Dameron has three holes in one to his credit and even makes his own clubs. He didn't have a physical until he was 83. When asked why he didn't fill out a medical history report for the doctor, Dameron simply said, "There's nothing to tell."

When asked the secret to his longevity, he joked, "I eat whatever I want, and I stay out of doctor's offices." It didn't hurt that he quit smoking when he was 19.

Next up he has his eyes set on beating a record held by Harold Hoyt Stilson Sr., who at age 101 became the oldest golfer to record a hole-in-one.

"I have been very blessed," said Dameron, "So God willing, I'll still be playing when I'm 101."

I don't know about you, but I can get rather excited about playing golf with such a man. Perhaps those who shoot their age do so partly because they don't act it.

—◆—

I will sing to the LORD all my life; I will sing praise to my God as long as I live. May my meditation be pleasing to him, as I rejoice in the LORD.
PSALM 104:33-34 NIV

Question of the Day: What older person do I admire? Why?

Tip of the Day: Don't give way to the sin of comparison. You may never have a drive like the lean and lanky instructor on the DVD. Do your best and leave it at that. Even Tiger loses. Ask yourself what will matter a year from now. Five years from now. A hundred years from now. Practice lots. Smile even more. Work with what God gave you.

25

Top Twenty Golf Songs

My favorite hobbies are fishing,
hunting, and swimming. But
enough about my golf game."
BOB HOPE

I don't know about you, but I suffer from attention deficit—um...let me see...oh yes—disorder. So after writing the last chapter, I decided it was time to leave the office. Out on the course, I got to talking with my son and a couple golfing buddies about songs that were undoubtedly written on the trials and joys of golf. Now, the general population thought these hits were about other things. That's okay. We'll let them think so. But we who golf know better. See if you can add to my list.

1. Dire Straits: "Sultans of Swing"
2. Pat Benatar: "Hit Me with Your Best Shot"
3. Jerry Lee Lewis: "A Whole Lotta Shakin' Goin' On"

4. Hank Williams Jr.: "Your Cheatin' Heart"
5. Aerosmith: "I Don't Want to Miss a Thing"
6. The Beach Boys: "Good Vibrations"
7. Simon and Garfunkel: "Bridge over Troubled Water"
8. Elvis Presley: "All Shook Up"
9. Bob Dylan: "Blowin' in the Wind"
10. Herman's Hermits: "There's a Kind of Hush"
11. Patsy Cline: "I Fall to Pieces"
12. Porter Wagoner: "Green, Green Grass of Home"
13. Ray Price: "Born to Lose"
14. AC/DC: "Shot Down in Flames"
15. Willie Nelson: "Blue Eyes Crying in the Rain"
16. The Beatles: "The Fool on the Hill"
17. Abba: "The Winner Takes It All"
18. Movie soundtrack: "Hope Floats"
19. Aerosmith: "Get a Grip"
20. Harry Connick Jr.: "One Last Pitch"

And the favorite song after 18 holes? "(Might as well) Go for a Soda" by Kim Mitchell. No such list is complete, of course, without a few songs that were translated from other languages only to have the words mixed up. Like these...

Johnny Cash: "I Walk the Creek"
The Beatles: "Can't Buy Me Par"
Bruce Springsteen: "Born for the PGA"
The Temptations: "May I Have This Stance?"
Rod Stewart: "Some Guys Sink All Their Putts"

I hope you're able to laugh a little when you golf. I hope the jokes are better than these. Regardless, I've found that laughter sure beats counseling. Here are a few of the random questions that help me smile when I golf.

- Why is it that the easiest putt to hole out is my fourth one?
- Why are really lousy players the most likely to share with me their ideas about my swing?
- Why is it that I can hit the wide fairway 10 percent of the time and a one-inch poplar branch 90 percent of the time?
- Why do bunkers beckon and fairways repel?
- Why are so few of us born with the natural ability to hit the ball and so many of us born with the ability to throw a club?
- Why do I always replace my divot after making a perfect approach shot?
- Why, when there are two balls in a bunker, is mine the one in the footprint?

Humorist Will Rogers said of Bob Hope that he celebrated his one hundredth birthday thanks to golf and laughter. "I ain't so sure golf contributes to longevity," he explained, "but any golfer that can't laugh at his own game would be well advised to write an early epitaph."

A few thousand years before the advent of golf, God brought the Israelites out of captivity and back to Jerusalem. The psalmist tells what happened: "Our mouths were filled with laughter, our

Now you know... Fun on the golf course can certainly be carried too far. Comedian Buddy Hackett was known as an incorrigible prankster on the course. One day while golfing with fellow comedian Mickey Marvin, Hackett traipsed into the woods to look for a lost ball. "It took him a real long time," recalled Marvin. "He finally came out—completely naked. When I asked what happened to his clothes, he yelled, 'Locusts! It was locusts!'"

tongues with songs of joy. Then it was said among the nations, 'The LORD has done great things for them'" (Psalm 126:2 NIV).

I hope you're able to laugh a little when you play golf. Our golf partners and the world around us need to see our joy, don't you think?

I've always figured that a round of golf during which I did not laugh was a round when someone stuffed a handkerchief down my throat and tied me up, because I usually find myself laughing at some point—regardless of my score. Of course I get deadly serious sometimes. But I've discovered that I rarely record a respectable score when I'm not smiling often, thanking God for the beauty all around me, and yes, even humming one of those golf songs.

Remember, one of the fundamentals of golf is fun.

—∞—

Always be full of joy in the Lord. I say it again— rejoice!

PHILIPPIANS 4:4

Question of the Day: What is one good thing I can rejoice about today? Can I think of another song?

Tip of the Day: When on the driving range, spend an inordinate amount of time aiming at the 150-yard marker. Those who do find they develop the confidence to hit the middle of the green and are rarely down in more than three from 150 yards. Don't practice putting on the driving range.

26

Back into Play

Seve Ballestero *was asked to describe his four-putt at Augusta's Number 16 years ago. He said, "I miss. I miss. I miss. I make."*

We read the Bible and talked about why I've been struggling. My husband said, "You've got the game, but you're too afraid of messing it up." So I came out today and I just had fun.

Minny Yeo, LPGA star, after matching her career best at 68

My friend Vance finds pro sports boring. He calls hockey a sedative. He believes it's right up there with watching the shopping channel in black and white with the mute button on. I've tried everything to help him, but it's bigger than me. The guy needs counseling.

I keep reminding him of those transcendent moments of sport. Mike Weir's playoff victory at the 2003 Masters. Kirk Gibson limping the bases after his Cinderella home run in the 1998 World Series. The time Tiger Woods hit the guy in the gallery on the head with a Nike ball.

I've told Vance that even Hollywood can't scare up the unbelievable endings that are enshrined in sports lore. He reminds me of the problems:

The greed of the owners.

The selfishness of the players.

The endless stream of marketing and merchandizing.

The escalating ticket prices.

The gambling.

The steroids.

The idol worship.

The price of hot dogs.

"It ain't a game anymore," he says. "Wake up and smell the decaf. Did you know that back in the good old days the Yankees paid Babe Ruth $80,000? The Americans paid President Hoover $5000. Something's rotten in Sportsland."

Sadly, I must admit that he has a point. The game is no longer a game. The ugliness of a National Hockey League strike turned the sports section into a gossip tabloid. Last month our local paper debuted a daily feature in the sports section. It's called "Who's in Trouble Today." The column looks like a bulletin board in an Old West post office—it's jammed with a never-ending list of culprits. One vendor at Shea Stadium was heard yelling, "Get your programs! Names and numbers of all the millionaires!"

I grew up collecting baseball and hockey cards. I'm not sure where they all went, but I loved lining them up on the floor and listening to *Hockey Night in Canada* blaring from a huge Philco radio. As I played with those cards, I dreamed of the day I would play with the big guys. But the years have given way to realism. Though I now count several professional athletes among my friends, the game I once thought existed seems gone forever.

I wonder sometimes if the devil isn't happy that we've managed to suck the play out of sport, that we've allowed business moguls to use a mere game to license entertainment and greed.

Perhaps that's why I love a round of golf with friends. I love the ribbing I take when I pull an illegal club from my bag. I love teeing it up with my sons and lunging at the ball in some faint hope that I'll be able to hit one as far as they do. I love to play at golf.

Play was God's idea, wasn't it? He planted Adam and Eve in a garden, surrounding them with greens and fruit and uninterrupted joy. It was the devil's idea that things take such a deadly serious twist, that play be corrupted. I'm not saying that life will be endless play; there is work to do. But as surely as I love to hear my children laugh as they build a sand castle, so God must take delight in our moments of play. Psalm 33 tells us how pleased He is when we play our musical instruments in praise to Him. Perhaps we can make our golf clubs sing too.

We are in this "valley of tears," snowed in by obligations and smothered by suffering. Where do we find the briefest glimpse of heaven while we are here? Where do we get a foretaste of the joy to come? C.S. Lewis provided an answer worth thinking about:

> It is only in our "hours-off," only in our moments of permitted festivity, that we find an analogy. Dance and game *are* frivolous, unimportant down here; for "down here" is not their natural place. Here they are a moment's rest from the life we were placed here to live. But in this world everything is upside down. That which, if it could be prolonged here, would be a truancy, is likest that which in a better country is the End of ends. Joy is the serious business of Heaven.

Since my father's passing I've been thinking more about this kingdom of joy that is to come.

And so my sons and I have begun playing golf with my dad sometimes. We call it Grandpa Golf. Here's how it's played. We add him as an imaginary fourth player. I have often joked that Dad was part Scotch and part Ginger Ale until God got His hands on him (it's true), so we pretend that since my Scottish father went to heaven, he is a far more incredible golfer than ever he was on this earth.

Grandpa is amazing now that he's truly golfing with the Master, and though his putts aren't great, his drives are impeccable. For instance, on a par 5, he will drive the ball 480 yards within ten feet of the hole, then four putt. On par 3s he sometimes duffs ten feet off the tee, duffs it again to within 150 yards, and then chips in for par.

One by one we take turns with Grandpa as a partner in a match against the other two, who play as a team. Thankfully,

I am still at the age where Dad and I can win most of the matches.

Like Vance, I give measured loyalty to professional sports now. I appreciate the unwavering discipline and skill it takes to earn a berth in the final foursome on Sunday at the Masters. Yet I always watch with a nagging sense of sadness as if something pure has been tarnished.

But put me on a golf course with amateurs, and I'll show you the one place in a fast-forward world where we actually push pause and play. The one place where we're given a tiny glimpse of the joyful kingdom to come.

—⁓⁓—

Friends, this world is not your home, so don't make yourselves cozy in it. Don't indulge your ego at the expense of your soul.

1 PETER 2:11 MSG

Question of the Day: When was the last time I pushed "pause" and "play"? When will I do so again?

Tip of the Day: Count every stroke, always. Bob Hope joked, "Isn't it fun to go out on the course and lie in the sun?" But when we lie, we cheat not only our partners but ourselves. I'd rather get an honest 104 and try to beat it than write down 84 knowing I never will.

27

Never Give Up

*They throw their clubs backwards, and
that's wrong. You should always throw a
club ahead of you so that you don't have to
walk any extra distance to get it.*
TOMMY BOLT ON THE TEMPERS
OF MODERN PLAYERS

*Actually, the only time I ever took out
a 1-iron was to kill a tarantula.
And it took a 7 to do that.*
JIM MURRAY

It's been one of those days on the course when hitting a
golf ball with a golf club was like playing the mandolin with a
tennis racket. Driving the fairway was about as easy as driving
a golf cart down the interstate. My favorite club in the sand
trap was a rake. For the first time in weeks I had the dreadful
inclination to throw my clubs in the creek. To walk off the
course. To call it quits.

Golf is a fascinating game, I tell myself. So fascinating that it's taken me 35 years to discover that I don't want to play it ever again.

How bad was my round? When I got home today, I sat down and penned this immortal poem. I have never done such a thing in my life, and I hope I never have to do it again.

Seventy-Two

I've stood before on the eighteenth green
    my gaze downcast and low.
For I'd dreamed the dream of seventy-two,
    then hit a nine or so.

I can kick the ball from tee to green
    in four and sometimes three.
But to do it with these dreadful clubs
    is an impossibility.

I can crank a ball three hundred yards
    when no one's there to see.
But I shank a ball three fairways right
    when someone's watching me.

And so I stand on the eighteenth tee
    with lofty visions high.
And dream the dream of seventy-two,
    three partners standing by.

I'm living well and eating right,
    I've repented when I've sinned.
I study books and DVDs,
    I've even prayed for wind.

And so I stare the flagstick down,
    my muscles taut with fear.
I try to shut the doubters out,
    those whispers in my ear.

I've cherished thoughts of seventy-two,
    but daylight's come and gone.
And I've yet to reach that golden goal
    my heart was set upon.

For I took a drive and topped the ball
    into some dreadful ditch.
I tossed a club into the woods
    I stifled language rich.

And then I landed out of bounds,
    then bounced one off a tree.
I'm lying now beside the cup.
    Tapping in for ninety-three.

Sometimes golf is a little like a school-yard romance. It's no fun if you don't take it seriously. But when you do, look out. It smiles at first. It leads you on. Then it gossips about you and runs off with one of your friends.

At such times it's helpful to remind myself that…well, that I have expensive clubs. That my wife bought them for me—with my money—so I shouldn't chuck them out. It's also helpful to remind myself that I am not the first one to consider quitting this awful game.

Even the greats are frustrated at times. Lee Trevino wrote, "I'm not saying my golf game went bad, but if I grew tomatoes, they'd come up sliced." One enormously frustrated hacker advised, "Real golfers, no matter what the provocation, never strike a caddie with the driver. The sand wedge is far more effective."

Countless examples exist of those who could have quit.

Albert Einstein was four before he spoke a word. (I know parents who would love this problem, but most wouldn't.)

Isaac Newton was considered unpromising in school.

When Thomas Edison was young, his teacher told him he was "too stupid to learn anything."

F.W. Woolworth got a job in a dry goods store at 21 but was not permitted to wait on customers. His boss said he "didn't have enough sense to close a sale."

Walt Disney was fired by a newspaper editor because he "lacked imagination and had no original ideas."

Michael Jordan was cut from his high school basketball team.

Babe Ruth struck out 1300 times, a major league record.

John Hudson grew up with an alcoholic father and determined to get out of the house whenever he could. That's when John took up golf. By the age of 16 he was shooting par with borrowed clubs and was told he could turn it into a lucrative career. Working evenings and weekends at a local mill, John finally earned enough to buy the best set Wilson made. But two days later they went missing. His

> **Now you know...** The record holder for dogged determination in the world of golf just may be held by Ian Baker-Finch. He missed 34 consecutive cuts. His most embarrassing moment came at the 1995 British Open at St. Andrews. While paired with Arnold Palmer, he hooked his drive out of bounds on what is considered the widest fairway on earth. Soon he quit competitive golf and now analyzes it on ABC Sports.

father had sold them for a hundred bucks—to buy money for booze.

John never bought another set. He never golfed another round.

All his life that set of clubs had been a metaphor for defeat. All his life he had believed his father's lies that he would never amount to anything.

Past tears, John, now 70, told me his story after I spoke at a fundraiser. "I'll be taking it up again," he smiled. Past the failure and regret, he had decided to press on.

I love how C.S. Lewis put it:

> No amount of falls will really undo us if we keep on picking ourselves up each time. We shall of course be very muddy and tattered children by the time we reach home. But the bathrooms are all ready, the towels put out, and the clean clothes in the airing cupboard. The only fatal thing is to lose one's temper and give it up.

For Winston Churchill, life didn't get off to a great start. Born in the ladies' room during a dance, he went on to fail the sixth grade. In one of his most famous speeches, he said, "Never give in. Never give in. Never, never, never, never—in nothing, great or small, large or petty—never give in, except to convictions of honor and good sense."

He went on to smoke more than 300,000 cigars during his 90 years of life.

Tomorrow, I'll take Winston Churchill's advice. No, I won't take up smoking. But I will get back out there. Just think. If I live to be 93, I can shoot my age.

—m—

Therefore, since we are surrounded by such a great cloud of witnesses, let us throw off everything that hinders and the sin that so easily entangles, and let us run with perseverance the race marked out for us.

HEBREWS 12:1 NIV

Question of the Day: Have I quit something that I need to take up again?

Tip of the Day: To cure a hook, Harvey Penick advises that you make "the Vs of one or both hands point at your chin. When one cures a hook by putting the left hand too much on top of the club, it is only a matter of time before the swing gets out and over the ball. In your swing, concentrate on clipping the tee or brushing the grass. This will take the club straight through."

28

Unbreakable

*I always thought of myself as some sort of
athlete until I started playing golf a couple
of years ago.*
JAMES CAAN, ACTOR

*Golf is not a wrestle with Bogey; it is not a
struggle with your mortal foe, it is a physi-
ological, psychological, and moral fight with
your self; it is a test of mastery over self; and
the ultimate and irreducible element of the
game is to determine which of the players is
the more worthy combatant.*
ARNOLD HAULTAIN, AUTHOR AND POET

My son Jeffrey and I were at a tournament where we found
ourselves paired with a lawyer and a stock car racer. I kid you
not. The guy in the clubhouse made the mistake of giving us a

cart that was faster than his. At 15, my son could not have been happier. All this stock car racer could do was swing his club at us as we sped past.

Between the laughter, the lawyer was telling us sad stories of working with young offenders. Then he said something remarkable: "I have yet to defend a young man in court who was an avid golfer."

I was trying to putt at the time, and it threw me off a little.

"Kids who grow up playing golf learn to follow a rule book," he explained. "They learn discipline, respect, and etiquette."

Someone on the tee box behind yelled at us to hurry up, but the lawyer wasn't through.

"They learn that you are responsible for your mistakes. To repair your divots. That there are absolutes."

Mark Roe and Jesper Parnevik can tell you about absolutes. During the 2003 British Open, the two were supposed to exchange cards on the first tee but forgot. Roe mistakenly signed Parnevik's scorecard. Both were disqualified from the tournament.

Even touching a golf ball between the time it's teed up and the time it is holed out was once an infraction. Just ask golf pro Lloyd Mangum. During a playoff at the 1950 U.S. Open, a stubborn bug attached itself to Mangrum's golf ball and couldn't be shooed away. Mangrum picked it up and blew on the bug. He was assessed a two-stroke penalty, thereby blowing his chances to beat Ben Hogan.

And then there's Aaron Baddeley, who showed up a mere forty seconds late for his tee time at the start of round two of the 2003 PGA Championship at Oak Hill Country Club in Rochester, New York. Penalized two strokes, he began a swift decent down the leader board.

I'm sure each of these would like to rewrite some rules. And they're not alone. If I were in charge, the rules would look something like this:

1. Since I've not had time to warm up, on the first tee I shall employ Driving Range Rule number one, shooting until I have reached my full potential.

2. A ball in the water is temporarily out of service. I have been punished enough by losing it, so I will close my eyes, throw a replacement at the green, and hit it again.

3. Whether or not a ball is out of bounds depends on the level of danger associated with playing it. If I perceive that there may be snakes, guard dogs, or burrs that may cling to my shorts, the ball shall be replayed. Besides, the pros have people to look for theirs.

What's true in golf is often true in life. All around us people are trying to rewrite the ancient Rule Book to read that the single greatest sin is intolerance. That there are no absolutes, that whatever you want is fine, just don't hurt anyone. But could it be that God's laws exist not only for our protection but for our pleasure?

On the last day of the golf season, a friend and I decided we would set our own course. With not a soul in sight, we teed off on number three and aimed for number six. We then headed for two from eight, then back to four. It was a dreadful experiment. I lost more balls in four holes than I did all summer.

My friend Ed Wallan knows what happens when we write

our own rules. Living in 24 different homes by the time he was old enough to join the coast guard, his earliest memories are filled with fighting, yelling, and crying—all that accompanies alcohol abuse. In first grade he began skipping school to visit the zoo—studying zoology, he claimed. Before long he was on a first-name basis with the cops, and his mother sent him to live with his dad and his third wife. One awful night his drunken father and a buddy staggered down the railway tracks and ran into an oncoming train.

After second grade Ed was banished to a camp for wards of the court and then shuffled from house to house. One family belonged to a cult that told him there was no such thing as sin or pain or death. "I was certain there was sin," he recalls, "I'd felt pain, and I knew about death too."

Following high school, Ed visited his grandma while waiting for a posting with the coast guard. There he watched Billy Graham on TV. He was fascinated by the gospel, but he knew that becoming a Christian would cramp his lifestyle.

"God didn't let me get far though," he remembers. "The only Christian I knew in the coast guard had his bunk next to mine."

Completing military service, he went to see a buddy from high school and was shocked to see a Bible beneath his arm. In an attempt to run, he set goals for himself: Get a job, a new car, and a wife. He reached all three. Almost. After a fit of anger, he exploded at his fiancée. When she returned her diamond, he stomped out of her house, threw the ring as far as he could, quit his job, sold his car, and took off for Portland, Oregon, to live with an aunt.

On the way, he sat down beside an old gentleman in a café. Turning to Ed, the man said kindly, "Son, do you know the Lord?"

"Wow!" thought Ed, "They're everywhere."

He arrived at his aunt's early Sunday morning. Guess what she had in her hand? A Bible and Sunday school material. "Let's go to church," she said.

"Am I the only one going to hell?" he wondered.

In a meeting a few nights later, Ed was sitting by the aisle ready to escape when he heard the same invitation Billy Graham had given years before. But he was stubborn. Suddenly he felt a tap on the shoulder and a whisper: "You'd better come to Jesus, Son."

"Why am I hanging onto my old life when God offers me His love and forgiveness?" wondered Ed. That night he did something he has never been sorry for. He invited Jesus Christ to be his Savior and Master.

I wish you could golf with Ed. No one has more fun being lousy at it. Now the pastor of a large church, he is one of the most joyous men I know. When he leaves a message on my answering machine, I get down on the floor because I'll be there laughing sooner or later anyway.

Ed knows enough to keep one hand on the Rule Book and the other reaching up for God's grace. He knows two irrefutable laws of living well:

Only when we hunger and thirst for things we cannot eat and drink will we be satisfied.

And we'll never experience true freedom until we live in obedience to the greatest Rule Book of all.

—∞—

If you love me, you will obey what I command.
JOHN 14:15

Question of the Day: In what ways will obedience bring me freedom and joy?

Tip of the Day: After a bad shot, try freeze-framing your follow-through and holding it until the ball comes to a rest. Don't pose too long, of course. But short-game guru Dave Pelz believes this allows you to self-analyze what you've done, recognizing the crucial differences between good and bad swings. He says some of his students still prefer throwing their club.

29

The Missing Peace

It's almost impossible to remember how tragic a place this world is when one is playing golf.
ROBERT LYND

Most golfers I know love golf partly because they love to get away from it all. They love to leave the noise and bustle and busyness of life in hopes of discovering a quieter place. A place where they can forget their stress, if only for a few hours. The golf course lures us with promises of stillness, of solitude, of peace, doesn't it? Sometimes it delivers, of course. And sometimes, well, sometimes it falls woefully short.

We all have our horror stories. Let me tell you mine. Recently, on a 150-yard par 3, I hit the creek four times with my 8-iron. I did this in style. I bounced one. I sliced another. I hooked a third. And the fourth almost made it—I'm being truthful—but it sounded like one of those thin rocks we threw into rivers when we were kids. *Shoop.* It was gone. I was golfing with friends at the time. Former friends, I should say. These friends knew all the rules of golf. In fact, one happened to be carrying a rule book in his bag. He pointed out that I was smacking my ninth shot before I even stepped off the tee box. I briefly considered smacking him with my ball retriever. But golf is not a contact sport.

Though my surroundings were tranquil, serene, and harmonic, there was nothing peaceful within me. Nothing made me say, "Boy, isn't this relaxing? Let's go 36 holes today." The truth is, golfing with friends can be a lot like learning to play the bagpipes in public. You open yourself to criticism, the odd snicker, and perhaps an incoming tomato or two.

I kicked my bag a little too hard that day, and as I limped to hit my tenth shot, I began to think of other things that were in my life. Turbulent things. Things that made me wonder where I could go to find the missing peace. And though I love pristine fairways and sloping greens, I reminded myself that peace is not found in a place—it is found in a person.

Peace may be the most sought after and elusive treasure of the ages. A French historian computed that during the last 3500 years mankind has known only 227 years of peace. That's 15 years of war for every year of harmony. Our world is characterized by fear. *Time* magazine recently titled a cover story "What Scares You Most?" Psychologists chart phobias now from A to Z. Everything from arachibutyrophobia (fear of peanut butter sticking to the roof of your mouth) to zemmiphobia (fear of the great mole rat). There's even pentheraphobia (fear of your mother-in-law) and bogeyphobia (which isn't the fear of golf but sounds like it should be!).

When you are truly living and golfing with the Master, you know that He is the Prince of Peace. Christ alone enables us to have peace with God by His work of reconciliation. I have watched over and over in my life as He resolves inner conflicts and tensions that threaten to rob my peace of mind. When Isaiah wrote the verse at the end of this chapter, he was given the gift of expectancy. We are given an even greater gift, I believe. We are given the experience of Christ.

God Himself promises us perfect peace. The words are translated from the Hebrew word *shalom,* a beautiful word often used as a farewell phrase, meaning well-being and abiding peace. Is it really possible? Can we experience peace in the midst of tragedy and terrorism and turmoil? Can we really know God's perfect peace despite the problems and challenges—the ample sand traps and wide creeks—that invade our lives?

Yes.

Christians through the ages have experienced it when they have listened to the Master's voice: "Peace, be still."

With its golf package, one travel agency promises "peace of mind." A SAAB car advertisement boasts, "Peace of mind starts at $299 a month." But the secret of true inner peace is not found in the right place or the right car but in our steadfast trust in God. Though we hit the creek with a pocketful of balls, though we have to hire a rubber raft and a scuba suit to find them all, remember this: We cannot drift beyond God's love and care.

—〰—

You will keep in perfect peace all who trust in you,
whose thoughts are fixed on you!
ISAIAH 26:3

Question of the Day: What do I need to trust
God for today?

Tip of the Day: Golf rules allow you to mark your
golf balls in any way that will give you an advantage.
Some are helped by marking balls with a straight
arrow to help align their swing path on the tee or
on the green. I once golfed with a man who had
somehow printed a likeness of his boss on the ball. I
do not recommend this.

30

Promising Hazards

Golf is a day spent in a round of strenuous idleness.
WILLIAM WORDSWORTH

But you don't have to go up in the stands and play your foul balls. I do.
SAM SNEAD, TO TED WILLIAMS,
ARGUING WHICH WAS MORE DIFFICULT TO HIT—
A MOVING BASEBALL OR A STATIONARY GOLF BALL

Every golfer knows someone who measures the success of his golf game not by how low his score plummets but by how many balls he has found during a round. It is a new handicapping system. "I'm plus eight!" no longer means you are eight strokes over par, it means you found eight more balls than you lost. It matters not how scuffed or scraggly the balls are, each one counts, and finding them has become more desirous to the golfer than working on his or her game.

My friend Scratch can't understand people like this. The moment you toss a ball retriever into your bag, you've given up on golf, he thinks. It's only a matter of time before you've packed it in altogether and are standing in the middle of the creek with hip waders, a lunch pail, and a ball catcher.

I was critical of such folk until recently when Ron, Vance, and I took our families for a weekend getaway to a resort called Panorama—which just happened to have one of the highest-ranked courses in Canada a pitching wedge from our chalet. When we arrived and drove slowly past the course, our wives rolled their eyes a little. No, they rolled them a lot.

"We're not going to play golf," we insisted.

They didn't believe us.

"We'll make brunch every morning," we promised.

They knew we were lying.

"We'll chop wood," volunteered Ron.

I punched him hard on the shoulder.

But in a rare moment of bad judgment, we had already decided that we wouldn't golf. We would romance our wives. I know you're surprised. I was too.

And sure enough, early the next morning we guys woke to light the fire and crack open the eggs.

First, however, we thought we'd better go for a short walk and get a breath of fresh air. Since we needed walking sticks, I rummaged around the trunk of the car, and wouldn't you know it, I found a few short irons and a ball retriever. Ron brought along some plastic grocery bags. In the wilderness, you can never be overprepared.

Frost had blanketed the greens during the night, so we made our way along a cart path until we came to a kidney-shaped pool of shallow water that wrapped itself halfway around a green. Along the cart path the pool was picked clean, but when we walked around to the back, we could not believe our eyes. The floor of the pond was littered with hundreds of balls within easy reach.

We began scooping them up like madmen. One of us excitedly shoveled while another bagged and the other hollered directions.

The original plan was to walk a hundred yards and hit them back into the pond, but we noticed something. People who golf at such resorts don't use old scuffed-up balls. They use Titleist ProVs. So we kept fishing and bagging and hollering.

Ron mentioned that a submerged ball loses half its carrying power, but we didn't care. I reasoned that it's an urban legend started by golf courses to keep slow golfers moving. Besides, I can hit a waterlogged ball just as far into the rough as a brand-new one.

As we scrambled and scooped, I suddenly noticed that Vance was not helping. I was about to say something when I saw him staring wide-eyed into the distance.

"Hey, look," he said.

Ron and I stopped fishing and raised our heads.

Ragged edges of sunlight had peeped over the mountains behind us, lighting up the snowcapped peaks, turning them a brilliant rosy red. The autumn trees below remained subdued in the predawn shade, awaiting the light. As the pond settled into quietness, the entire scene was mirrored in the water and framed by the silver frost on the fairway and green on the other side.

It was one of the most beautiful sights I have ever seen.

I wish I could tell you we went back to the chalet for a camera or our wives. We did not. We kept scooping like madmen and then lugged our booty back to the chalet while our families were still snoring.

There we cleaned our treasures in the kitchen sink. And counted them. Guess how many. Four hundred and eighty balls. I kid you not.

As we scrubbed the mud off each and every one, I looked out the window above the sink at the mountain scenery and then back at my hands in the murky water. And I told the others a story my mother told me after I found a quarter one day when I was a boy.

It was the story of a man who found a five-dollar bill in a gutter and spent the rest of his life looking for more. According to my mother, he never saw the trees. He never saw the flowers. He never saw the birds. In fact, he missed a hundred rainbows and a thousand sunsets. All he saw was gutters.

"Always look a little higher," said my mother.

Ron and Vance seemed to agree. "Tell you what," I said. "I'll keep these balls, so you won't get too attached to them. And I'll go soak in the scenery. You make us some brunch."

―〰―

Lift your eyes and look to the heavens: Who created all these? He who brings out the starry host one by one, and calls them each by name. Because of his great power and mighty strength, not one of them is missing.

ISAIAH 40:26

Question of the Day: What is something I miss seeing when I sweat the small stuff?

Tip of the Day: Aim at the top of the flagstick. Former touring pro and skills instructor Wally Armstrong says that many amateurs come up short of the pin during their approach shots because they try to land the green and roll their ball toward the hole. Afraid of overshooting the pin, their muscles tense, and they come up short. Keep your head down but aim high.

31

To the Dogs

*My favorite shots are the practice swing
and the conceded putt. The rest can never be
mastered.*

LORD ROBERTSON

My wife and I took the dog along to the course the other day. It's not something you'd get away with in most places, but with the (forgive me) dog days of summer a distant memory and winter fast approaching, I knew it was okay. Apart from two other diehards five or six holes ahead of us, we had the course to ourselves.

"Sit!" I commanded her (my dog, of course) whenever I took a swing. And she sat. Other than that Mojo was free to roam, rousting out gophers, cocking her head at a lone muskrat chewing some weeds along the creek bank.

Watching her, I decided that dogs would find golf an easy

game. In fact, I'm surprised they haven't taken over this sport completely and purged us humans from the record books.

For one thing, dogs are better prepared mentally. Mojo rarely has a care in the world. She wouldn't let bad shots bother her for a minute. Once I got mad at her for chewing a new ProV golf ball of mine, and the next thing I knew she had weaseled her way back onto my lap with a lick of my hand and a wag of her tail.

Imagine taking that attitude onto the golf course. You'd smack an errant drive into a bunker and dive in after it with gusto, happily blasting it onto the green. You'd shank one into the woods and bound in there like you couldn't wait, smiling all the while, wagging your tail, sniffing in eager anticipation.

It's not like there's a lot on your mind. There is no pressing assignment, no cell phone ringing, no one you have to call. You might think of snacks or buried bones back home, but that's about it.

As you stand on the tee box, your tongue hanging a little to the left, you turn around three times and punch the ball out there straight and true.

Dogs would never lay up. They would go for it and make it every time. They wouldn't know they couldn't.

Dogs would kill us if they took up this sport.

Cats, on the other hand, would not do so well. They are an indifferent lot, easily bored. Dogs say, "Let's go, let's hurry, come on, pant pant pant." They thrive on repetition.

Not cats.

Cats shoot par once and they never need to play the sport again. If they showed up at all, they would spend their time in the pro shop preening themselves, disapproving of other golfers' bad outfits. If they made it to the course they would be a nuisance. Cats would give new meaning to "scratch golfer." They'd be penalized for slow play, and they wouldn't care. They'd refuse to wear soft spikes. Cats would cheat. They would sit on the line of your putt and refuse to move. They'd sooner die than go near a water hazard. And you definitely wouldn't want them close to a sand trap.

When our children were small, I told them tales of Mojo the Super Dog, the hound of my youth. I spun yarns of her undying devotion, of how she bravely rescued children from burning buildings and how she was a pro golfer, winning the grand slam twice. When finally we got a dog of our own, our children would consider only one name: Mojo. Within a week they taught her to sit, to lay down, and to shake with the wrong paw. Though she's never learned to golf, she's taught me a few tricks that have come in handy on the golf course. Here they are:

1. Wag the right thing.

Perhaps a dog is called "man's best friend" because he wags his tail, not his tongue. Sadly, the golf course can be notorious for gossip. It can be a place where we tear others down. One of the best rules I've ever established for myself on a golf course is that if I talk about others, I will do so as if they were present. Proverbs 16:28 warns, "A troublemaker plants seeds of strife; gossip separates the best of friends." First Thessalonians 5:11 advises, "So encourage each other and build each other up, just as you are already doing." Wag the right thing.

2. Stay away from the rocking chair.

Sometimes at night, with Mojo at my feet, I read the

newspaper and find myself talking out loud. I say things like "I wonder about the situation in the Middle East," and she's thinking, "I sure wish he'd put down the paper and open up a can of tuna." A good dog knows that newspapers are useful for certain things but that worry is like a rocking chair. It gives you something to do, but it doesn't take you anywhere. The great thinker Yogi Berra once said, "Ninety percent of the game is half mental." Focusing on our worries and fears can destroy a round of golf, so stay away from the rocking chair.

3. Keep your head up.

It's bad golf advice I know, but when my son came through the front door recently, I could tell how he'd done on the golf course. But Mojo didn't care. She met him at the door with her tongue ready. She ran in circles, leaping in the air and licking his face as if it were aging cheese. Mojo didn't ask how many bogeys he shot, she just loved him.

As my son stood to his feet, a bright smile lit up his face. And I couldn't help thinking that even a furry little creature can reflect its Creator with undying love and devotion that gives us bright hope and every reason to carry on.

I need some of that love right now. You see, my wife is calling. It seems Mojo II just discovered the toe of one of my golf shoes.

—∾—

May the words of my mouth and the thoughts of my heart be pleasing to you, O LORD, my rock and my redeemer.

PSALM 19:14

Question of the Day: What results have I witnessed when I "wag the right thing?"

Tip of the Day: Forget the gimme. Oh, I know they're nice, but learn to tap in those short putts—it will help you in tournament play. Vance tells me a gimme can best be defined as an agreement between two golfers, neither of whom can putt very well. And he's usually right. If a friend offers you a gimme in a close match, thank him and then step up and miss by six feet.

32

Divine Mulligans

One of the most fascinating things about golf is how it reflects the cycle of life. No matter what you shoot, the next day you have to go back to the first tee and begin all over again and make yourself into something.

PETER JACOBSEN

Grace grows best in winter.

SAMUEL RUTHERFORD, SCOTTISH PREACHER
(1600–1661)

One terrible day in late October, when the last of the leaves has turned color and kissed the branches goodbye, when the course has been aerated, leaving fairways cluttered with hunks of dirt and sand traps littered with multicolored foliage, my buddies and I extend to each other uncommon grace, permitting the demolition of golf's most sacred statute: Play it as it lies.

It seems sacrilegious to hard-core golfers but not to us. With snow fast approaching, we are sometimes forced to wear numerous layers of cumbersome sweaters and unsightly mittens, which constrict one's normally fluid movements. Therefore we play "winter rules." They look roughly like this.

- Balls may be raked from bunkers.
- And kicked from behind trees.
- They may be lifted, cleaned, dropped, and adjusted until the golfer is satisfied.
- There shall be no such thing as a lost ball. The ball is merely missing and will eventually be found and pocketed by someone else. You are therefore warranted a free drop or a do-over.
- Next time someone should bring hot chocolate.

We've played snow golf a few times, a wonderful winter diversion during which we extend even more of this grace to one another. We bring pink, orange, or yellow balls, unless the snow has begun to drift, in which case the color doesn't much matter. I hold the uncontested course record for the longest drive—well over 700 yards—something I accomplished by bringing the creek into play. The ball makes more of a *thunk* than a

Now you know... Nome, Alaska hosts the annual Bering Sea Ice Golf Classic. Golfers play six holes with the frozen sea beneath. They use spent shotgun shells as tees and old coffee cans buried in the ice for holes. Among the interesting local rules is one that allows for score adjustment in the event a polar bear comes into play. Add three strokes if one grabs your ball. Subtract five if you get it back.

ping when the club, the ball, and the golfer are all frozen, and if you hope to hit it again, it is necessary to peel your hat off and listen for the sound of the ball dropping on the fairway.

The sheer implausibility of hitting a good shot makes us cheer for each one like never before. "Come on," we say, "hit another one," words rarely uttered in the dead of July.

During these six- or seven-hole outings, I can't help thinking of grace. You see, the game of golf has been a constant reminder of my shortcomings. I duff. I fail. I stumble. I fall. Yet the grace of God comes along and changes everything. This unmerited favor, this love that stoops and rescues the likes of me, is the Master's greatest gift.

I'm so thankful that God says, "You'll never measure up, so accept the gift of grace from One who did. It's the one key that will unlock heaven's door." Listen to these liberating words of grace: "Because of the sacrifice of the Messiah, his blood poured out on the altar of the Cross, we're a free people—free of penalties and punishments chalked up by all our misdeeds. And not just barely free, either. *Abundantly* free!" (Ephesians 1:7-8 MSG).

Have you ever wondered what would happen if certain Bible characters sent letters of application for ministry positions in a church? Would the Thursday night search committee meeting sound something like this?

> "Let's talk about this Adam."
> "Well, he seems like a good man, but he takes bad directions from his wife. And you don't even want to know what he wears in the woods."
> "How about Noah?"

"He's prone to taking on huge building projects without a permit. He's a pessimist too."

"What about Joseph?"

"Brags too much. Has a prison record. He's even been accused of adultery."

"And Moses?"

"Are you kidding? He's a lousy communicator. He stutters and stammers. He has a bad temper and has been known to hit things with a stick."

"So he's a golfer then?"

"That's another of his shortcomings."

"What do you know about Job?"

"Well, he's loaded, so he won't need a salary. But he's pretty gloomy. He complains too much."

"David looks like he has promise."

"Yes, but his kids are out of control, and his wives are a handful. To make matters worse, he's a strong proponent of instrumental music in worship."

"Tell me about Solomon."

"Well, he has a good head on his shoulders, but he's got problems when it comes to building projects. It took him seven years to complete the temple and thirteen years to build his palace. I guess he was trying to please all those wives."

"What about Elijah?"

"No way. Prone to depression. Collapses under pressure. Spends too much time by himself in the wilderness."

"And Samson?"

"Hair's too long."

"Jonah?"

"Good runner, but he makes up big fish tales. Has been disobedient to God."

"Matthew?"

"Not a chance. Works for the IRS."

"What about this John the Baptist?"

"He sure doesn't dress like a Baptist. Strange diet. Makes the Pharisees mad."

"And Peter?"

"Bad temper. Curses sometimes. Claims to have visions."

"Paul?"

"Powerful preacher and a good leader. But he's short on tact and has been known to preach all night. Puts people to sleep. Controversial on women's issues. He's single too."

"What about these others on the list?"

"Lazarus is dead."

"Zacchaeus is too short."

"Timothy is way too young."

"Methusaleh is too old."

"Sarah laughed too much."

"What about Judas?"

"Well, let's talk about him. He comes with good character references. Good connections. He's conservative, so he won't rock the boat. Handles money well. Maybe he's the one."

Aren't you glad God in His mercy chose to use the likes of these? They literally shaped the course of human history. And He will do it again through you. All of us have sinned. But we don't have to live with the guilt. When we truly repent, God forgives and restores us to favor.

Recently a friend of mine offered me a gimme putt from three feet. I declined—and two-putted! History's greatest gimme is the gift of eternal life offered through Jesus Christ. All we need to do is accept it and pass it along.

Let the rules of winter golf remind us to give thanks for the divine mulligan of grace.

—⁊⁊—

He saved us, not because of the good things we did, but because of his mercy.

TITUS 3:5

Question of the Day: Whom do I need to show grace to today?

Tip of the Day: If you tend to slice the ball, tee the ball up on the right-hand side of the tee box and then aim toward the left side of the fairway. If you tend to hit the ball from right to left, do the opposite. For a banana slice you can set your watch to, drop your back shoulder coming through.

33

Thanksgiving in August

Now, here's Jack Lemmon, about to play an all-important eighth shot.
JIM MCKAY, ANNOUNCER

If you don't drive a golf ball at least 268 yards, you will need the U.S. Navy on your left and the French Foreign Legion on the right.
SPORTS WRITER EDWIN POPE, DESCRIBING NUMBER 18 AT THE DORAL-RYDER OPEN

It was seniors' night on the golf course, and three widow ladies were about to tee off. A good-looking younger gentleman approached and asked if he could join them. Immediately they perked up.

"You're new here, aren't you?" asked one of them.

"I moved to town this morning," he answered pleasantly.

The second lady grinned shyly. "Where did you live before you moved here?"

"San Quentin. I spent the last 20 years in prison."

The first two shrank back. But not the third lady. "What were you in for?" she asked.

"I murdered my wife."

She smiled brightly. "Oh," she said, "so you're single?"

Have you ever noticed that different people see things in different ways? It's all about perspective, I guess.

On August 31, 2005, 80 percent of New Orleans was underwater, devastated by Hurricane Katrina. My brother-in-law Lauren and I flipped past the golf channel and spent the evening watching the news as rescuers and residents along the Gulf Coast struggled to cope with the horrifying destruction. Lauren, a television news photographer who has seen horrors I've only read about, was deeply touched as a "hardened" colleague choked back tears while trying to describe the devastation. "It's like a third world country," she said.

My wife, who at the age of eight watched her own father drown in a flood, watched with empathy.

The next morning Lauren and I arose early, ate the one breakfast I can prepare (toast), and headed for the golf course. Our surroundings bore a startling contrast to the images on

TV. In the midst of the flat prairies, a network of lush green spread its fingers across the valley, beckoning hackers like us. The sun blazed as we walked beside the gentle creek.

We spoke of the very first time we played golf together among the tall pines of a pristine mountain course in British Columbia. I laughed as I described a shot Lauren had taken with a 5-iron. Once smacked, the ball commenced to take a miraculous right angle turn and enter the woods. Until then I had no idea a ball could ricochet off that many trees after being hit only once. Turning to Lauren, I saw him acting as if he were having a stroke himself.

Holding his club as if it were an axe, he took his frustration out on the grass, yelling, "What in the…Doh! Aooh! Dog biscuits!" Or something similar.

This day beside the gentle creek his game was no better.

Lauren's slice had returned with a vengeance. His putts bounced, his chips rolled.

Yet he did not utter a word.

No smacking the fairway. No griping. No hollering.

When I asked him why, he just smiled.

"Things could be worse," he said. "We could be in New Orleans."

Perspective. It makes all the difference.

According to scholars, perspective is the art of seeing. But true perspective is far more than sight. It is the foundation on which we stand, the filter through which we see life. It is our worldview.

Someone has said that you become what you behold. If that is true, then maybe the golf course is one of a very few places that afford us a view worth beholding. We live in a noisy culture saturated with instant messaging and cell phone parenting. Frankly, there is ample bellowing but little beholding.

A quiet game of golf can frustrate the life out of me or remind me of all the things I have to be thankful for.

What are you seeing?

Is your golf slice your biggest problem? Or are you aware that 98 percent of humans will never hold a club?

During a trip to a third world country we ran out of bottled water one day, and my parched mouth began to speak to me loudly, dictating my every whim. Never in my 40 years of life had I experienced such raging thirst, and though I've never had to deal with alcoholism, I suspect it is a similar sensation. The urge to have a drink consumed my entire attention. There were few things I wouldn't have given up or done in exchange for one small sip.

In a tiny village not far from a plush golf course, a dear and blessed saint of a lady opened a small icebox and presented me with the greatest treasure imaginable: an ice-cold bottle of Coca-Cola. I felt like a drowning man who had been thrown a sturdy rope and pulled aboard the Queen Mary.

I held that bottle up to the light to admire its color.

I stroked it and cradled it and giggled like a fourth grader at recess.

I sipped it slowly, relishing every single drop as it crawled down my eager throat.

I have tasted Coca-Cola since, and I wonder why they no longer use that recipe. This drink was nectar straight from heaven. It was not only a friend, it was a teacher. And this is what it taught me:

When I am disillusioned and tired and cynical, a sense of wonder often returns when I ask myself, what if I never experience this again? Supposing this dreary round with a cranky partner and a set of clubs I'd like to throw in the creek is my last one? What if I never again watch a sunset, or hold my sleeping child, or enjoy a meal with friends? Let me give thanks today. Let me savor these things while I still have them within my grasp.

—✳—

I will praise you, O Lord, with all my heart; I will tell of all your wonders. I will be glad and rejoice in you; I will sing praise to your name, O Most High.
PSALM 9:1-2 NIV

Question of the Day: What is something I haven't "savored" enough lately, but need to?

Tip of the Day: Take dead aim. When you hit the ball you shouldn't hear other voices. Think not on what is going on around you, on who is watching or the awfulness of your last shot, but on where you want the ball to end up. Take dead aim. Golf is an easy little game. It's like writing. You just concentrate until sweat blurs your vision.

34

Best Round Ever

*If your opponent is playing several shots in
vain attempts to extricate himself from a
bunker, do not stand near him and audibly
count his strokes. It would be justifiable
homicide if he wound up his pitiable exhibi-
tion by applying his niblick to your head.*

HARRY VARDON

I've had some bad rounds of golf. And some good ones too.
But only one thus far would I dub as truly great.

We'd been playing golf together since he was barely able
to lift a club. And we'd both grown by leaps and bounds. Not
only had we seen one of our scores plummet dramatically, my
partner had put on 100 pounds. You've probably guessed. He
is my firstborn son.

There was a time when I almost gave up golfing with him.

You see, my boys got so mad at each other I considered getting them Nerf clubs. The way they fought over rules, scores, duffed shots, and whether or not someone coughed when they were shooting was legendary.

I remember the par 3 where Jeffrey hit the creek. He took it hard enough, but when his brother whispered, "Sploosh," it pushed him over the edge. There was yelling. And threatening. And more yelling.

I didn't take the whole thing so well either, but I've begun to realize that all of us need a training ground, a safe environment where we can encounter the fact that we are died-in-the-wool sinners. For me and my boys, this has been the golf course.

With the permission of my son, I have reprinted a letter I handed him one night following a miserable round. You can read it, and I'm sure you'll be able to read between the lines.

> Dear Stephen,
>
> I hope you know you are one of the most important people in the world to me. I also hope you will give me a minute of your time. I was frustrated with you on the golf course today. You got mad and complained, and it made things miserable for your brother and me.
>
> I'm sorry if I spoke too harshly. I was frustrated too. I should have remained silent. It's something I'm learning. Would you please allow me to offer some advice? When golfing, try not to take it so seriously. You may never play the game professionally, nor will I. There are only six kinds of golfers: pros, those who have fun, those who are

constantly frustrated, and those who can't count. Mostly I'm in the second category. But we can't let it get to us.

Here's my suggestion: Count five steamboats after each swing. After the final steamboat, do your best to grin and think of the next shot. I just read of a pro in Britain who took a 19 on one hole. Kid you not. Think of him. Think of ice cream. If this doesn't work, chuck your clubs in the air. Not really. Don't do that. Don't chuck your brother's clubs either.

More than any of these things, honor others and apologize when you're wrong. I will gladly relinquish my car keys to you when you do.

I hope we can golf together until long past the time I am old. I won't even cry when you beat me. I promise. May all your shots be straight, your drives long, and your putts short. May your ball lie in green pastures, not in still waters. And may you follow our precious Jesus through every bunker and trap that life throws your way.

Cheering you on,
Dad

One September day Stephen's mother and I waved goodbye as this boy left for Bible college. I winced a little when he told me his plans. You see, this wasn't on my agenda for him. I've checked *Fortune 500* and *Money* magazine. There are very few ministers and missionaries listed there. I asked my wife, "Who's gonna pay for my medication when I reach retirement?" She didn't know.

That night we crawled into bed, my wife and I, the lawn neatly trimmed, the house cleaned, the back porch swept, and she said, "Aren't you glad Stephen wants to serve God? We've prayed that he would since he was knee-high to a Lego block." How could I disagree?

Most nights after we finish a round of golf, Stephen brushes his teeth outside our bedroom door. If the door is open, he comes in. Boys are easy to talk to when there's toothpaste in their mouth. Suddenly I missed those talks. I missed him thumping down the stairs and pretending he wiped out, just to see the horrified looks on our faces. I missed the music he would crank up about 11 PM in the room below us. Even if it sounded like someone killing chickens with a jackhammer. I missed him rolling on the floor with the dog and sometimes me and standing at the fridge together about midnight talking of our round and wondering where Mom hid the mayonnaise.

Even the dog misses him.

I went looking for Mojo tonight. She was lying on Stephen's bed, her tail in the downward position. And try as I might to be brave and manly and a positive thinker Robert H. Schuller would admire, there were tears coming down my cheeks there in the dark.

I know there are far worse things than hugging your firstborn goodbye as he goes off to Bible college, but I miss my son.

"Lord," I prayed, "take care of this boy. I know he

> **Now you know...**Mike Corns had seven witnesses when he aced the 349-yard par 4 at Eagle Crest outside San Diego—in his bare feet...with a range ball. So he summoned members of the media and took 16 more cracks at it. He failed to sink one but did get one ball within a foot of the cup.

was on loan, but we got pretty attached to him. Wherever he is and wherever he goes, go with him."

God heard that prayer. In fact, something happened as he studied God's Word and interacted with others. God grabbed hold of the boy. Gave him purpose. Filled him with hope.

The next spring when he returned for the summer, we found ourselves playing golf again. And he was a changed boy.

Between shots Stephen told me what God was doing in the deepest parts of his soul.

"I'm planning on working in Uganda, Dad. At an AIDS hospice. I want God to use me."

I said, "Are you sure you want to do that? Why don't you just stay in North America and be comfortable?" He grinned. He knew I was joking. Since the child was old enough to listen he'd traveled with me, listening to me preach about sacrifice and laying our lives down for the sake of others.

I have always been proud of my children. But never before had I given thanks to God in tears for what He was doing in their lives. For a son who's willing to go to any lengths to make a difference.

And at the end we tallied up our scores, and they were remarkable. I gave thanks for that too. And I thanked God that He loaned us two more kids. They're bright kids. They'll make good doctors and lawyers. They can buy my medication.

—∞—

Teach me your way, O LORD; lead me in a straight path.

PSALM 27:11 NIV

Question of the Day: Since I am made to last forever, what is something temporary I should sacrifice to invest in the eternal?

Tip of the Day: Take as much care to line up a four-footer as you would a ten-footer. A four-foot miss counts just as many strokes as a 300-yard drive. Who said golf is fair?

35

Independence Day

*I never pray to God to make a putt. I pray
to God to help me react good if I miss a putt.*
CHI CHI RODRIGUEZ

*If you wish to hide your character, do not
play golf.*
PERCEY BOOMER

When my wife and I were first married, we were introduced
to a remarkable man by the name of Larry Burkett through a
video series on managing your money. Among other things
we learned to budget and to do something incredibly radical:
spend less than we make.

I didn't know at the time that Larry was an avid golfer.

Best known for his popular radio program "Money Matters," which is broadcast on more than 1100 stations, Larry

wrote more than 70 books with more than 11 million copies in print.

In March, 1995, Larry, his wife Judy, and their four children were stunned to learn he had renal cell carcinoma (or kidney cancer) that had spread to his left shoulder blade. The fact that his golfing days were over was the least of their concerns. The cancer was deadly. Ninety-five percent of those with his type of cancer die within two years, he was told. Burkett underwent two surgeries, one to remove a kidney and a second to remove his shoulder blade. Though his cancer was in remission, Larry lived with chronic pain.

Researching the disease on the Internet, he began to explore alternative therapies, learning he could not access them until they met FDA approval. So he fought and changed the law in Georgia and seven other states so that alternative therapy can now be given if administered by a licensed physician. When he learned of an immune therapy offered in Prague, he talked to ten others who took it and lived longer than expected. After undergoing the treatment, he made changes: He drank filtered and ozonated water. He ate white chicken meat, a little fish, and very little red meat.

After writing a book called *Making Life Rich Without Any Money*, I was asked to be on Larry's radio program. During a return visit, I was surprised to learn that he wanted to golf with me.

And so one humid fall day we hit the links together. Larry had no left shoulder blade, yet he made no excuses. His swing, though slightly awkward, was strong, and his drives were straight. "It hurts a little," he admitted, "but I've been building up the muscles around it."

I won't tell you our score that day, but after 18 holes we were tied. Rather than a quick playoff, we sat in an Applebee's restaurant together as Larry told me of his life. "God has been so good," he said several times.

"I was supposed to be gone five years ago," he smiled, scanning the chicken section of the menu, "but He must have something left for me to do."

"Are you ever angry?" I asked rather bluntly.

"No," he said. "I don't blame God, if that's what you mean. There must be a reason for all of this. People talk about dying gracefully. I'm focusing on getting well."

"What helps you do that?"

"I pray a lot, I read a lot, and I praise God a lot," he said. "That has made all the difference."

"Do you have any fears?" I asked.

"After my first cancer surgery, when they removed my right kidney, I awoke one night knowing that in two weeks I'd be returning to the hospital for the removal of my shoulder blade. I was full of fear. Suddenly I felt the presence of the Lord in that hospital room, and I heard a voice—not audibly—but in my spirit, saying, 'Have no fear. This is for the glory of God. Just do what God called you to do.' Fear is the opposite of faith," said Larry. "Faith is the belief in something greater than we are."

"So is the fear gone?"

He looked me in the eye. "I have no fear of dying," he said, and repeated it, "I have no fear of dying.

"After Senator Harold Hughes came to Christ, someone asked him, 'What is the advantage of being a Christian?' Hughes replied, 'This life is all of hell I shall ever experience.

The disadvantage of being an unbeliever is that this life is all the heaven some people will ever know. I was saved when I was 32. My only regret is that I didn't come to Him sooner.'"

"What will heaven be like?" I asked.

Larry smiled. "There will be no more cancer," he said. "No diabetes, heart trouble, overweight, wrinkles, or gray hair."

"Why are you looking at me?" I asked.

I shall never forget his laugh.

On July 4, Larry declared independence from his body.

I was on my way to the post office when his cohost, Steve Moore, called and told my wife that Larry was Home. Ironically, the cancer that had tested him for eight years did not take him—it was heart failure. At the post office I picked up a parcel, and back home I discovered that it was a personally inscribed copy of Larry's latest devotional book, *Great Is Thy Faithfulness*. The book is a treasured reminder of that round of golf with a humble servant of God. When I reminded Steve of that golf game, he said, "I guess you were the last one to golf with Larry."

Let me close with Larry's words:

> I've given some thought to what my epitaph should be, and I think I'd like my tombstone to read, "Larry Burkett, a servant of the Most High God."
>
> I just pray that at my death someone will be able to write that, legitimately.
>
> I don't know if people use epitaphs anymore, but if you died suddenly and your family wanted to write an epitaph for your gravestone, what do you think it would be?

Remember, the greatest epitaph will be the one given by Christ. What will He be able to write about you?

—⟋⟍—

Well done, good and faithful servant...enter into the joy of your master.

MATTHEW 25:21 RSV

Question of the Day: When I'm gone, what would I like said about me (besides "Look, he's back!")?

Tip of the Day: Be there. I'm not talking about tee times, though we both love those. I'm talking about the Ultimate Appointment. One day soon we will see our Master face-to-face. I can't wait to celebrate with you as we cast our crowns at His feet. Until then, let's live for His glory, in His presence, all the way Home.

36

Finishing Well

*Don't play too much golf. Two rounds a day
are plenty.*
HARRY VARDON

*Golf is deceptively simple and endlessly
complicated; it satisfies the soul and frus-
trates the intellect. It is at the same time
rewarding and maddening—and it is
without a doubt the greatest game ever
invented.*
ARNOLD PALMER

Some Monday in late October Jim aerates the fairways, tucks in the greens, and locks up the clubhouse. Most are resigned to the fact that winter is coming, but a few fanatics refuse to quit. They are out there now, whacking their golf balls at temporary greens. But as surely as every round of golf comes to an end, so does every golf season.

Out my window gray clouds circle, threatening to pelt us with snowflakes and weather so cold that even the polar bears will consider hibernating from it.

Every year I drag the clubs from the trunk of the car some chilly Saturday and spend a few hours indoors cleaning them up, tightening my cleats, and washing balls I've found. Then I store them away for five or six long, long months. My friends to the south ask if winter depresses the life out of me, and I tell them no, I'd probably golf less if I lived where they live because I wouldn't really appreciate what I have, I would take it for granted, all that stuff. It's a bald-faced lie, of course, but I'll probably tell it again this year. I like curling, I tell them, have you heard of it?

When I sat down to write this book, I prayed that God would use it to bless the reader and draw you closer to the Master. I have four more wishes as I close.

1. I hope you'll have fun at the game.

This summer we've been incorporating three new variations that have helped bring the fun back to golf. A time or two we've played One Throw, in which each player is forbidden to use his clubs for an entire hole. He must throw the ball instead. It is embarrassing how rarely he loses.

Another variation on golf is a game we call Yell. During the course of the match each player is allowed one bloodcurdling holler. It is not necessarily the best cure for the yips, but a round where Yell is played is one that is not soon forgotten. The key to Yell is twofold:

1. Ganging up on the leader.
2. Suspense.

The best yellers seem to teeter on the edge of yelling whenever the other players are about to hit the ball. They cough softly and take deep breaths. Last spring I could hold a forkful of potatoes at the dinner table without shaking a bit. This is no longer the case. Some chalk it up to age. I blame the little game we call Yell.

The third game and my personal favorite is called Reverse Mulligan. At some point during the match you are allowed to use one and only one reverse mulligan. If an opponent hits a ball from a fairway trap and sticks it two feet from the pin, or rolls one in from 46 feet, you can cheer, clap, and ask him to perform the miracle again.

Don't take this game too seriously. Practice your putts and chips (and your yell!), but remember to practice your laugh too.

2. I pray you'll hang onto hope.

Author Horace Hutchinson once joked, "If profanity had an influence on the flight of the ball, the game of golf would be played far better than it is." Contrary to what you may have heard on the course, the four-letter word that best describes golf is *hope*. Hope is the reason we crawl back onto the course after being humiliated in the way Rick Reilly of *Sports Illustrated* described so well when he wrote, "Golf is the cruelest game, because eventually it will drag you out in front of the whole school, take your lunch money and slap you around."

Why do we keep punching that tee into the ground and

cradling a ball on top of it, knowing we'll probably get slapped around? Because of hope. Because we get to thinking that maybe, just maybe something miraculous is about to take place. Maybe, just maybe this next shot, things will go right, and we'll be there to see it happen.

Golf is all about hope. And so is life. Perhaps hope can be defined as Having One Purpose: Eternity. Real hope vanquishes despair and dread and gives birth to faith. Hope is not some vain wish that all will be well; it is the knowledge that more surely than spring will come and those clubs will once again grace my trunk, the Master is risen from the dead and promises us eternity with Him.

3. I trust you'll pursue true success.

What will it take for you to consider yourself a success? I'd love to lower my score, but will that make me a success? I'm thankful God has allowed me to write books, but has that made me a success? How badly our culture has mangled the meaning of the word. It has become synonymous with stuff. Don't confuse fame with success. Tiger Woods achieved one. Billy Graham achieved the other. What does the Lord require of us? Micah 6:8 gives the answer: "The LORD has already told you what is good, and this is what he requires: to do what is right, to love mercy, and to walk humbly with your God."

I remember the day I received an e-mail from a man who had accepted Christ as his Savior and Lord after reading my little golf devotional. The sky was brighter than I'd seen it before. The trees were greener. And I knew I had been offered a tiny glimpse of what we will celebrate throughout eternity.

Perhaps true success is the glorious privilege of pointing others to Christ.

I once asked Jim Cymbala, pastor of the Brooklyn Tabernacle, a most unusual question: "When will you consider yourself a success?" He said, "When people hear one of my sermons and go away talking about me, I have failed. If they go away talking about Jesus, I've succeeded."

4. I hope you'll finish well.

Many nights while I was writing this book I would hop in my car and drive northward past a miserable little golf course that sucks the life out of my game to a hospital where my father sat in a fog called Alzheimer's. I tried to encourage him—with hugs mostly—and with kind words he didn't seem to understand. As I watched my parents say their slow goodbye, I was aware that the toughest chapter of life can be the last one. It is not an easy thing, to finish strong. But the rewards are out of this world.

I remember one night in particular, amid a one-sided conversation as I was running out of things to tell him, Dad's eyes suddenly lit up, and his mouth opened.

"Home," he said, past a beautiful smile.

My dad wasn't a great golfer, but he was a straight shooter. His life started out off course, but he finished well. A faded plaque hung in our hallway when I was a boy. I don't know where it ever went, but I'll not soon forget what it said: "Folly delights a man who lacks judgment, but a man of understanding keeps a straight course" (Proverbs 15:21 NIV). I think it's a golfer's verse.

The example of those who finish well is a powerful elixir

to those of us who come behind. My mother couldn't tell you which end of a golf club to hang onto, but she knows how to finish the course, how to hang onto hope.

Just yesterday a nurse told me that Mom always brightens her day with a smile and a kind word. When I said goodbye to her last night, I said, "God bless you, Mama," and she smiled upward.

"He already has," she said. "He gave me you."

And I knew I'm the richest grown-up kid alive.

One of my favorite golfers, without a doubt, is the apostle Paul. He said, "I have fought the good fight, I have finished the course, I have kept the faith."

May God give you the strength to finish strong. To keep the faith.

Let me close with another of my favorite golf verses from the book of Proverbs. It is my prayer for you as you close this book and walk with the Master:

> *Look straight ahead, and fix your eyes on what lies before you. Mark out a straight path for your feet; then stick to the path and stay safe. Don't get sidetracked; keep your feet from following evil.*
>
> 4:25-27

About the Author

Phil Callaway owns a set of Callaway clubs and a badly mangled Spaulding putter. He plays golf with his teenage sons and usually ends up paying for the round. His swing is consistently mediocre, but he managed to shave four strokes from his handicap by practicing what he preaches in this book. Phil speaks at golf tournaments, for corporations, churches, and conferences. He lives with his high school sweetheart, Ramona (they are married), who enjoys golf as much as Phil enjoys attending quilting bees. Phil's other books include *Making Life Rich Without Any Money*, *Who Put My Life on Fast Forward?*, *Wonders Never Cease*, and *Laughing Matters*. As he speaks and writes, his mission is to bring joy to life and to make others homesick for heaven. For more about Phil's ministry, or to check out his other books, CDs, and DVDs, visit www.philcallaway.com.

Also by
Phil Callaway

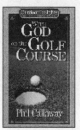

WITH GOD ON THE GOLF COURSE
Although Callaway offers no guarantee for a lower golf score, he does provide 40 short devotionals full of wisdom, grace, humor, and enjoyable reflections on the sport Mark Twain called "a good walk ruined."

MAKING LIFE RICH WITHOUT ANY MONEY
Find joy in what really matters! Columnist and speaker Phil Callaway identifies six characteristics of rich people—characteristics that have nothing to do with money and everything to do with wealth. Convenient mass-market size.

WHO PUT MY LIFE ON FAST-FORWARD?
Callaway's personal stories and those gleaned from millionaires, CEOs, and "regular folks so tired they can hardly lace their Velcro tennis shoes" show how God can help us live deliberately in a high-speed culture.

HARVEST HOUSE
PUBLISHERS

And You'll Love Phil's two Novels...

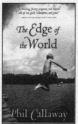

THE EDGE OF THE WORLD
When young Terry Anderson stumbles onto a hidden stash of money, his life suddenly comes to a crossroads. The mystery leads him to even more amazing discoveries in a town called Grace.

WONDERS NEVER CEASE
Eighteen-year-old Terry Anderson never expected to find a dead body. He had no idea that the gnarled fingers would pry open family secrets long buried and test every ounce of faith he ever had.

HARVEST HOUSE
PUBLISHERS